6/22/07 Bishop T. D. Jakes

TAKE the Anionting ♡

plAce where I stop believing GOD

Don't give up until GOD blesses me.

Ministries - Pastor, Women, Young ladies
    Marriage - Dwight
  House -

In the state of my blindness I Am still
growing.

To:

_____

From:

_____

About the Author

Best-selling author Karol Ladd offers lasting hope and biblical truth to women around the world through her positive book series. A gifted communicator and dynamic leader, Karol is founder and president of Positive Life Principles, Inc., a resource company offering strategies for success in both home and work. Her vivacious personality makes her a popular speaker to women's organizations, church groups, and corporate events. She is co-founder of a character-building club for young girls called USA Sonshine Girls and serves on several educational boards. Karol is a frequent guest on radio and television programs. Her most valued role is that of wife to Curt and mother to daughters Grace and Joy. Visit her Web site at PositiveLifePrinciples.com.

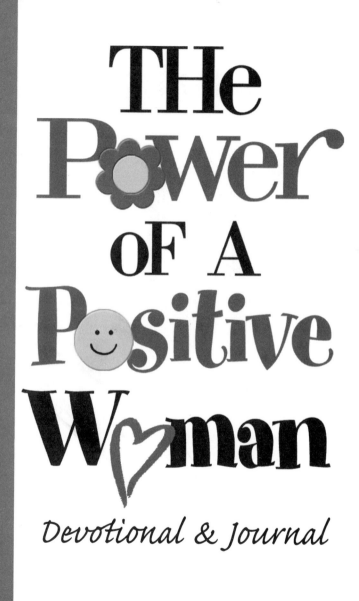

THe P⬤wer OF A P☺sitive W♥man

Devotional & Journal

Our purpose at Howard Books is to:

- *Increase* faith in the hearts of growing Christians
- *Inspire* holiness in the lives of believers
- *Instill* hope in the hearts of struggling people everywhere

Because He's coming again!

Published by Howard Books, a division of Simon & Schuster, Inc.
1230 Avenue of the Americas, New York, NY 10020
www.howardpublishing.com

The Power of a Positive Woman Devotional and Journal © 2007 by Karol Ladd

10 Digit ISBN: 1-58229-614-6; 13 Digit ISBN: 978-158229-614-2
10 Digit ISBN: 1-4165-3815-1; 13 Digit ISBN: 978-1-4165-3815-8

10 9 8 7 6 5 4 3 2 1

HOWARD colophon is a registered trademark of Simon & Schuster, Inc.

Manufactured in the United States of America

For information regarding special discounts for bulk purchases, please contact Simon & Schuster Special Sales at 1-800-456-6798 or business@simonandschuster.com.

Edited by Michele Buckingham
Cover design by Stephanie D. Walker
Interior design by John Mark Luke Designs

52 Monday Morning Motivations

THE Power OF A Positive Woman

Devotional & Journal

Karol Ladd

HOWARD BOOKS
A DIVISION OF SIMON & SCHUSTER
New York   London   Toronto   Sydney

Contents

Contents

Introduction

*We trust not because "a God" exists,
but because this God exists.*

C. S. Lewis

Welcome to a faith walk. Not a sprint or a jog, but a steady journey of strengthening your faith as you follow the steppingstones of God's Word.

Perhaps you picked up this book because you desire to be a more positive woman. Maybe you are already an upbeat sort of person, and you simply want to strengthen and encourage your heart. Either way, this devotional is created for you. It's designed to help you take a fresh faith walk through God's Word, learning practical and positive applications along the way. As you move through the pages, you will not only gain a positive perspective for your life, but you will also increase your faith in a loving, encouraging, and positive God. That's what this book has done for me as I've written it; my hope is that it will do the same for you.

To be honest, I'm not sure how positive I would be if I were left to my own devices. I'm a woman just like you. Most of us tend to defer to the negative in our thinking—a sort of default mode, especially when life gets tough. But here's what I've discovered: All of God's attributes are positive. And God's power is more than capable of turning our hearts in the positive direction of faith and hope!

The Power of a Positive Woman Devotional and Journal

Introduction

is a transforming book—not because it's filled with *my* amazing words, but because it's filled with principles that come from *God's* amazing Word, the Bible. As you will soon discover, each weekly faith-filled lesson is gleaned from a book in the Bible, beginning with Genesis and concluding with Revelation.

Within each weekly devotion you will find a key scripture, a positive reflection to apply to your life, encouraging quotes by heroes of the faith, a sample prayer you can use as a guide in your own prayer time, and a place for you to write your specific prayer needs for the week. I have also included several positive choices you may want to make in response to the devotion, as well as space to record any personal choices God places on your heart. Finally, I have offered a suggestion for further Scripture reading, so you can continue to dig deeper into God's Word.

This is a doable devotional. I'm guessing your schedule keeps you fairly busy. If you're like most women, life is filled with family, friends, work, church, appointments, commitments, requirements, and a myriad of other demands on your time. A Monday-morning devotional may be the perfect prescription for starting your week off in a positive, faith-filled direction. If Monday mornings don't work for you, try Monday nights. Or Tuesday mornings. The point is to find a time that's best for you, then stick to it on a weekly basis.

As I prayerfully wrote each week's devotion, I began to recognize an amazing, intricate theme running through the whole book—a beautiful scarlet thread tying it all together: the power of faith and the transforming work of Christ in

Introduction

our lives as women. My prayer is that as you spend this year walking step by step through God's Word, your faith will be increased, your love for God will be strengthened, and you will become a more positive woman through his amazing power.

Don't wait. Start this week. Start today! I'll be walking right alongside you, encouraging you through the words in this book. More importantly, God will be with you—just as he always is. I pray that his Holy Spirit will guide you every step of the way. Enjoy your walk with him. Take some time to hear what he is saying to you. Allow him to transform you into the positive, faith-filled woman he created you to be.

Stepping Out in Faith

Key Scripture: Genesis 12:1–4

The LORD had said to Abram, "Leave your country, your people and your father's household and go to the land I will show you.

I will make you into a great nation and I will bless you; I will make your name great, and you will be a blessing. I will bless those who bless you, and whoever curses you I will curse; and all peoples on earth will be blessed through you."

So Abram left, as the LORD had told him; and Lot went with him. Abram was seventy-five years old when he set out from Haran.

Faith will not always get for us what we want, but it will get what God wants us to have.

VANCE HAVNER

Stepping Out in Faith

 **Reflection**

What faith! God told Abram to leave the comfort of everything he had always known and go to a new place. How did Abram respond? How would you and I respond? Abram chose to step out and step up to God's calling. He traveled to new territory at the vibrant young age of seventy-five with God as his guide. Are you willing to follow God's call into unknown territory, even if it means leaving your comfort zone?

Personally, I prefer to dwell in a place of safety and comfort. I'm guessing you feel that way too. Yet there are times when God calls us out of the cozy and into an uncomfortable situation that stretches our faith and increases our dependence on him.

Stepping out in faith will look different in each of our lives. It may involve reaching out to a lonely neighbor or starting a Bible study or feeding the homeless or taking on a leadership role at church. One thing is for sure: as we hear God's call and step out in faith, we can trust him to be with us and to see us through.

Week 1

💡 My Thoughts

Am I listening for God's call in my life? What does he want me to do that may require me to step out in faith and away from my comfort zone? _Ministered to the_ _young ladies & women._ _Advertising business_

💜 My Prayer

"Great and mighty Lord, you know all things and can do all things. Help me to listen for your voice, and show me clearly what you want me to do. Give me the strength and faith to walk in obedience to your call. Thank you for your presence in my life. Thank you that I am never alone, because you are always with me. You are always leading me. I trust that whatever new territory you have prepared for me, you will guide me there and lead me through. In Jesus's name I pray, amen."

This week I am praying for: _The courage to_ _stand in what I know is right_ _gain Victory. I know that when_ _I am not in prayer things I let go._

Stepping Out in Faith

 My Choices

- This week I will choose to seek God's direction in my life.
- This week I will choose to step out in faith and obedience.
- This week I will choose to thank the Lord for his blessings and his presence in my life.
- This week I will choose to: _____

_____

_____

_____

_____

_____

 **For Further Reading:** Genesis 15

> Faith puts God between us
> and our circumstances.
>
> F. B. MEYER

God's Daily Provision

Key Scripture: Exodus 16:11–16

The LORD said to Moses, "I have heard the grumbling of the Israelites. Tell them, 'At twilight you will eat meat, and in the morning you will be filled with bread. Then you will know that I am the LORD your God.'"

That evening quail came and covered the camp, and in the morning there was a layer of dew around the camp. When the dew was gone, thin flakes like frost on the ground appeared on the desert floor. When the Israelites saw it, they said to each other, "What is it?" For they did not know what it was.

Moses said to them, "It is the bread the LORD has given you to eat. This is what the LORD has commanded: 'Each one is to gather as much as he needs. Take an omer for each person you have in your tent.'"

When you have nothing left but God, you become aware that he is enough.

AUTHOR UNKNOWN

God's Daily Provision

 **Reflection**

Day by day God provided for the needs of his people as they marched through the wilderness. God hasn't changed! He still provides for his people—you and me—day by day. But like the Israelites, we can easily fall into a habit of grumbling and despair, especially when life isn't going smoothly or we don't know what the future holds.

We must make a deliberate choice to turn to God and trust him for our daily needs. God wants to show us that he is our Lord and our provider, just as he showed the grumbling Israelites. Dear friend, don't let despair overtake your emotions! Instead, with faith, look to God for help and provision for this day. He can be trusted.

Week 2

My Thoughts

In what areas of my life do I need to relinquish despair and trust God for his provision? _____

_____

_____

_____

_____

_____

My Prayer

"Loving heavenly Father, I praise you, because you are my protector and my provider. Thank you for meeting my needs and watching over me day by day. I trust you, because you are able to do all things. You are all-sufficient. When I feel uncertain, help me to seek your help and provision instead of resorting to worry or despair. Strengthen my faith as you provide my daily bread. Thank you for all you have done and all you will do in my life. In Jesus's name I pray, amen."

This week I am praying for: _____

_____

_____

_____

_____

_____

God's Daily Provision

 My Choices

- This week I will choose to turn to prayer instead of despair.
- This week I will choose to trust God to provide for my daily needs.
- This week I will choose to praise God for being my protector and provider.
- This week I will choose to: _____

_____

_____

_____

_____

_____

For Further Reading: Exodus 16:1–36; 17:1–7

> When you have accomplished your daily task, go to sleep in peace; God is awake.
>
> Victor Hugo

The Power of Christ's Sacrifice

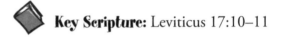 **Key Scripture:** Leviticus 17:10–11

Any Israelite or any alien living among them who eats any blood—I will set my face against that person who eats blood and will cut him off from his people. For the life of a creature is in the blood, and I have given it to you to make atonement for yourselves on the altar; it is the blood that makes atonement for one's life.

There can be no thought of "cheap" forgiveness when we remember that our redemption cost God the life of his beloved Son.

GEOFFREY B. WILSON

The Power of Christ's Sacrifice

 **Reflection**

Frankly, Leviticus is one of those books in the Bible most of us would rather skim over. Rules, rituals, observances, and instructions about sacrifices are not exactly pleasure-reading material. But the beauty of Leviticus is that it points to our need for Christ.

The Israelites were required to make continual animal sacrifices as payments for their sins. These sacrifices may seem like a bloody mess to us. But sin is serious business to God, and he requires serious payment. "It is the blood that makes atonement for one's life." For the Israelites, animal sacrifices were only temporary payments; to continue to receive God's forgiveness, they had to bring sacrifices to the altar over and over again.

The picture Leviticus sketches is one of sinful humanity in need of a permanent sacrifice. Jesus came to be that one and only permanent sacrifice—the final, perfect payment for the sins of the world. He completed the picture in rich and living color by laying down his life on the cross for you and for me. May each of us cherish in our hearts the wonder and beauty of what Christ has done for us!

💡 My Thoughts

Have I come to a point of faith in Christ's sacrifice on the cross for my sins? What difference does Christ's sacrifice make in my thoughts and actions? _____

_____

_____

_____

_____

_____

💙 My Prayer

"Glorious Lord, I praise you for your sacrificial love. Thank you for giving the world the gift of your Son, Jesus. Thank you for the power of Christ's blood that was shed on the cross for me. I'm grateful for his sacrifice that paid the penalty for my sin once and for all. May my words and actions reflect my gratitude for what Jesus has done for me! Give me the strength to forgive others as I have been forgiven. In Jesus's name I pray, amen."

This week I am praying for: _____

_____

_____

_____

_____

_____

The Power of Christ's Sacrifice

 My Choices

- This week I will choose to reflect on the great sacrifice Christ made for me on the cross.

- This week I will choose to thank the Lord for his mercy and forgiveness.

- This week I will choose to show God's grace and mercy toward others in my life.

- This week I will choose to: _____

_____

_____

_____

_____

_____

 **For Further Reading:** Hebrews 9:11–10:18

Christ hath crossed out the black
lines of our sin with the
red lines of his own blood.

THOMAS WATSON

Perspective Is Everything

 Key Scripture: Numbers 13:30–32

Then Caleb silenced the people before Moses and said, "We should go up and take possession of the land, for we can certainly do it."

But the men who had gone up with him said, "We can't attack those people; they are stronger than we are." And they spread among the Israelites a bad report about the land they had explored. They said, "The land we explored devours those living in it. All the people we saw there are of great size."

We have a God who delights in impossibilities.

ANDREW MURRAY

Perspective Is Everything

 **Reflection**

Isn't it amazing to see the vastly different perspectives people have in life? Caleb and his buddy, Joshua, looked at life with a God-centered point of view. They saw the giants in the land and believed, *Our God is bigger than those giants, and he will fight for us.* They trusted God to come through for them, just as he had done so many times before. God had promised to give the Israelites the land, and they trusted him to fulfill his promise.

The other men had a fear-filled perspective. Their eyes were myopically focused on the challenges in front of them. I guess they forgot what God had already done. They seemed to think they were going to have to fight this battle on their own. Unfortunately, the fear factor spread more quickly than the faith factor; before long, all of the Israelites were filled with the same we-can't-do-it attitude.

What giants are you facing in your life right now? Are you willing to seek God's help and ask him to give you the strength you need? Faith grows when our eyes are on the Lord and we trust him to do what we cannot do on our own. Fear grows when our eyes are on ourselves and we forget God is with us. Let's choose to keep our eyes on the almighty God who loves us and is with us always!

💡 My Thoughts

How do I view the challenges in my life right now? Am I looking at them through the perspective of God's ability or my inability?_____

_____

_____

_____

_____

_____

💗 My Prayer

"I praise you, wonderful, omnipotent God! You have all power and authority, and you can do all things. You are more than able to conquer my challenges and carry out your purpose and plan for my life. I trust you. When I become fearful, fill me with faith. When I am weak, be my strength. Help me to keep my eyes focused on you. I know you will never give me more than I can handle with your help. Thank you for never leaving me. I love you! In Jesus's name I pray, amen."

This week I am praying for: _____

_____

_____

_____

_____

_____

Perspective Is Everything

 My Choices

- This week I will choose to see God at work in my life.
- This week I will choose to stop focusing on what I can't do.
- This week I will choose to encourage other people's faith by my words and example.
- This week I will choose to: _____

_____

_____

_____

_____

_____

 **For Further Reading:** Numbers 13:1–33; 14:1–45

> Faith does not operate in the realm
> of the possible. There is no
> glory for God in that which is
> humanly possible. Faith begins
> where man's power ends.
>
> GEORGE MULLER

Saturated with God's Truth

 Key Scripture: Deuteronomy 6:4–9

Hear, O Israel: The LORD our God, the LORD is one. Love the LORD your God with all your heart and with all your soul and with all your strength. These commandments that I give you today are to be upon your hearts. Impress them on your children. Talk about them when you sit at home and when you walk along the road, when you lie down and when you get up. Tie them as symbols on your hands and bind them on your foreheads. Write them on the doorframes of your houses and on your gates.

The church has no greater need today than to fall in love with Jesus all over again.

VANCE HAVNER

Saturated with God's Truth

 **Reflection**

No nibbling allowed! No light dabbling! Our passage today suggests the Israelites were to *saturate* their lives with God's Word. His commands were to be on their hearts continually. The Israelites were to talk about them, teach their children about them, post them on the doorframes of their homes, and even tie them to their hands and foreheads.

Why did God instruct his people to keep his truth continually in the forefront of their thinking and conversation? Because it's so easy for us to ignore God and forget his words to us. We get busy, and our hearts begin to turn to other interests or pleasures. Pride sets in, and we begin to think we can accomplish everything on our own. If we fail to continually saturate our hearts and minds with God's truth, our faith becomes dry and our love for the Lord grows parched.

God wants us to love him with every part of our being; not just with our mouths, but with our hearts, our souls, and our strength. God isn't calling us to be so-so, once-a-week followers. He wants our lives to be saturated with him—overflowing with love for who he is and directed by the knowledge of how he wants us to live.

Week 5

💡 My Thoughts

How can I actively and practically saturate my life with God's truth? _____

_____

_____

_____

_____

_____

♡ My Prayer

"Gracious and loving Father, I praise you, because you are my creator and my God. Thank you for your great care for me. Thank you for your goodness. I confess that often I forget to look to you for help or thank you for all you have done. I desire to grow close to you and love you with all my being. Help me to keep my eyes fixed on you. May I never forget your faithful love for me! In Jesus's name I pray, amen."

This week I am praying for: _____

_____

_____

_____

_____

_____

Saturated with God's Truth

 My Choices

- This week I will choose to reflect and meditate on the attributes of God.

- This week I will choose to meditate on and memorize a passage from his Word.

- This week I will choose to talk about the attributes of God in conversations with my family and friends.

- This week I will choose to: _____

_____

_____

_____

_____

_____

 **For Further Reading:** Deuteronomy 6–8

> To cherish true love for God is to be
> constrained by love to yield one's
> ego with all that it is and has, and
> to let God be God again.
>
> ABRAHAM KUYPER

Remember God's Faithfulness

 **Key Scripture:** Joshua 4:4–7

So Joshua called together the twelve men he had appointed from the Israelites, one from each tribe, and said to them, "Go over before the ark of the LORD your God into the middle of the Jordan. Each of you is to take up a stone on his shoulder, according to the number of the tribes of the Israelites, to serve as a sign among you. In the future, when your children ask you, 'What do these stones mean?' tell them that the flow of the Jordan was cut off before the ark of the covenant of the LORD. When it crossed the Jordan, the waters of the Jordan were cut off. These stones are to be a memorial to the people of Israel forever."

O Thou who hast given us so much, mercifully grant us one more thing—a grateful heart.

GEORGE HERBERT

Remember God's Faithfulness

 **Reflection**

Don't you wish you could have been there when the priests, wearing their weighty sacramental garments and carrying the heavy Ark of the Covenant, first touched the Jordan River with their feet? What a step of faith that must have been for them! At that very moment, the Lord caused the water from the river to stop flowing, and the Israelites were able to walk across the dry riverbed to the Promised Land. What a marvelous, faith-building experience for the Israelites to remember!

Just as the priests were instructed to gather twelve stones and build a memorial to what God had done at the Jordan, so the Bible encourages each of us to remember and reflect on what God has done in our lives. OK, so maybe you haven't experienced anything as dramatic as the parting of a river, but I'm sure you've had times in your life when you've recognized God's miraculous hand at work. Maybe the miracle was a friend who showed up during a difficult time; an encouraging conversation; a sudden change in circumstances; an unexpected job opportunity. Let's be faithful to remember God's blessings in our lives—big or small—and look for ways to share the stories of his provision with others.

Week 6

My Thoughts

What are some ways I have seen God's hand at work in my life within the last few years? _____

_____

_____

_____

_____

_____

My Prayer

"God of all creation, I praise you for your marvelous works and your mighty miracles. You are the great and mighty God. Thank you for your love, care, and provision in my life. Thank you for the blessings you have given me. Thank you especially for _____. Help me to recognize the powerful ways you work in my life every day. Thank you for being with me and watching over me. In Jesus's name I pray, amen."

This week I am praying for: _____

_____

_____

_____

_____

_____

Remember God's Faithfulness

 **My Choices**

- This week I will choose to reflect on what God has done in my life.

- This week I will choose to seek God's help and direction when I don't see any solutions in sight.

- This week I will choose to encourage someone else's faith by sharing what God has done for me.

- This week I will choose to: _____

_____

_____

_____

_____

_____

 **For Further Reading:** Joshua 4; 6

> Gratitude to God makes even a
> temporal blessing a taste of heaven.
>
> WILLIAM ROMAINE

The Power of a Courageous Woman

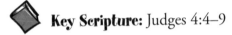 **Key Scripture:** Judges 4:4–9

Deborah, a prophetess, . . . was leading Israel at that time. She held court . . . and the Israelites came to her to have their disputes decided. She sent for Barak . . . and said to him, "The LORD, the God of Israel, commands you: 'Go, take with you ten thousand men of Naphtali and Zebulun and lead the way to Mount Tabor. I will lure Sisera, the commander of Jabin's army, with his chariots and his troops to the Kishon River and give him into your hands.'"

Barak said to her, "If you go with me, I will go; but if you don't go with me, I won't go."

"Very well," Deborah said, "I will go with you. But because of the way you are going about this, the honor will not be yours, for the LORD will hand Sisera over to a woman."

The remarkable thing about fearing God is that when you fear God you fear nothing else, whereas if you do not fear God you fear everything else. —OSWALD CHAMBERS

The Power of a Courageous Woman

 **Reflection**

A woman leading Israel? That may not sound surprising to us today; but in the early days of Israel, a woman in a position of government leadership was very unusual. We see from this passage that Deborah was both wise and courageous, and she trusted the Lord for guidance and strength. These were the qualities that made her a great leader.

God's plan is never constrained by race, gender, age, or status. He uses willing and faithful hearts to carry out his purposes. Barak was fearful, but Deborah was faithful. She rose to the challenge of leadership and lived beyond cultural expectations. As a result, Israel experienced a great victory. Never underestimate what God can do through a courageous woman who follows his leading!

💡 My Thoughts

What has God equipped me to do? Am I courageously moving forward, trusting him to help me every step of the way?

_____

_____

_____

_____

_____

💗 My Prayer

"Holy and perfect God, I praise you, because you work in miraculous and unexpected ways! I trust you to lead me and work through me. You know my heart and my potential, and you have a plan and a purpose for my life. Thank you for using Deborah in a unique way, and thank you for the example she sets for women everywhere. Use me in a unique way as well. Help me to listen to you and obey you. Give me the courage to follow you, wherever you lead. In Jesus's name I pray, amen."

This week I am praying for: _____

_____

_____

_____

_____

_____

The Power of a Courageous Woman

 My Choices

- This week I will choose to courageously follow God's leading and direction in my life.

- This week I will choose to recognize and value the unique potential God has placed in each person in my life.

- This week I will choose to think outside the box and be open to new and unique opportunities the Lord puts in front of me.

- This week I will choose to: _____

_____

_____

_____

_____

 **For Further Reading:** Judges 4–5

> Give us grace, O God, to dare to do the deed which we well know cries to be done. Let us not hesitate because of ease, or the words of men's mouths, or our own lives.
>
> W. E. B. DuBois

Famous for Faith

 **Key Scripture:** Ruth 2:11–12

Boaz replied [to Ruth], "I've been told all about what you have done for your mother-in-law since the death of your husband—how you left your father and mother and your homeland and came to live with a people you did not know before. May the LORD repay you for what you have done. May you be richly rewarded by the LORD, the God of Israel, under whose wings you have come to take refuge."

A kind heart is a fountain of gladness, making everything in its vicinity freshen into smiles.

WASHINGTON IRVING

Famous for Faith

 Reflection

Have you ever wondered what people think of you or say about you behind your back? Apparently people noticed Ruth and spoke very favorably of her. Imagine that! Instead of spreading negative gossip, the townspeople talked about Ruth's kindness to her mother-in-law and her faithfulness to God. How refreshing to see that her faith was the talk of the town. Although she wasn't trying to be showy, Ruth's actions shone brightly to the people of the city.

Certainly we don't want to do things just so people will look at us favorably; but Ruth's example spurs us to consider, What do people see in us? When people look at you, do they see a woman overflowing with faith and kindness, or do they see a woman who is caught up in worry and self-centeredness? I love how Boaz complimented Ruth by saying, "May you be richly rewarded by the LORD . . . under whose wings you have come to take refuge." Do you see the beautiful word picture here of Ruth finding her security in the love and care of the Lord? Oh, dear friend, may people see the same evidence of a beautiful and strong faith in your life and mine!

Week 8

💡 My Thoughts

Is a genuine, heartfelt kindness for others and faithfulness to the Lord evident in my life? _____

_____

_____

_____

_____

_____

💗 My Prayer

"Faithful Father, I praise you, because you are my provider and my protector. I am so glad I can take refuge under your wings, just as Ruth did! Thank you for blessing me in so many ways and continuing to provide for me day by day. Grant me a portion of your loving-kindness to pour out to the people around me. May my life reflect your love and faithfulness. Give me the direction and strength I need to minister to others. In Jesus's name I pray, amen."

This week I am praying for: _____

_____

_____

_____

_____

_____

Famous for Faith

 ## My Choices

- This week I will choose to build up others with my words, recognizing their good qualities.
- This week I will choose to reach out in kindness to the people around me.
- This week I will choose to find my refuge under the wings of God's faithful love.
- This week I will choose: _____

_____

_____

_____

_____

_____

 ## For Further Reading: Ruth 4

All right believing in God is
visibly reflected in right
behaviour towards men.

GEOFFREY B. WILSON

Beyond Appearances

 **Key Scripture:** 1 Samuel 16:6–7

When they arrived, Samuel saw Eliab and thought, "Surely the LORD's anointed stands here before the LORD."

But the LORD said to Samuel, "Do not consider his appearance or his height, for I have rejected him. The LORD does not look at the things man looks at. Man looks at the outward appearance, but the LORD looks at the heart."

The one thing God is after is character.

OSWALD CHAMBERS

Beyond Appearances

🌸 Reflection

How easy it is to look at another woman and begin to size her up by her appearance! Although we know it's not right, we often fail to look past a person's outer veneer to see her heart. Maybe the woman is a gorgeous, fashion-model type who we are certain is shallow. Maybe she's a sloppy, ditzy type who we assume doesn't have her act together. Either way, by making a quick judgment based on exterior factors, we are in danger of overlooking the real person inside. It takes godly wisdom and deliberate determination to look further than the surface and see into a person's heart. May the Lord give us "heart-eyes" to see beyond appearances!

Even more, may he give us grace to reflect on a more personal question: what does God see when he looks at *our* hearts? Certainly it's not wrong for a woman to attend to her appearance, but "looking perfect" should never be our central focus. Growing in character and in the knowledge of God's Word brings out a beauty far beyond skin-deep. Let's make sure our beauty on the inside shines brighter than our beauty on the outside!

💡 My Thoughts

Do I tend to focus more on outward appearances than on people's hearts? In what ways am I developing a beautiful heart of my own? _____

_____

_____

_____

_____

_____

💗 My Prayer

"Gracious and loving God, I praise you, because you are the God who sees all things. You see my heart, and you alone know what is really there. Forgive me, Father, for the ugliness in my heart. Gently and patiently create in me a clean heart and renew a right spirit within me. Help me to grow more and more in love with you and your Word every day. Give me "heart-eyes" to see beyond outward appearances to the real people underneath the facades. Grant me a heart of love toward everyone you have created. In Jesus's name I pray, amen."

This week I am praying for: _____

_____

_____

_____

_____

Beyond Appearances

 ## My Choices

- This week I will choose to ask God to renew my heart with his qualities of gentleness, kindness, and love.

- This week I will choose to look beyond appearances to people's hearts.

- This week I will choose to draw close to God through prayer and spend time in his Word each day.

- This week I will choose: _____

_____

_____

_____

_____

_____

 For Further Reading: Psalms 19:14; 51:7–12;
Proverbs 31:10–31

> Men in general judge more from
> appearances than from reality.
> All men have eyes, but few
> have the gift of penetration.
>
> Niccolò Machiavelli

Seeking Divine Wisdom

 **Key Scripture:** 1 Kings 3:7–10

*"Now, O L*ORD *my God, you have made your servant king in place of my father David. But I am only a little child and do not know how to carry out my duties. Your servant is here among the people you have chosen, a great people, too numerous to count or number. So give your servant a discerning heart to govern your people and to distinguish between right and wrong. For who is able to govern this great people of yours?"*

The Lord was pleased that Solomon had asked for this.

It is better to get wisdom than gold. Gold is another's, yet wisdom is our own; gold is for the body and time, wisdom for the soul and eternity.

MATTHEW HENRY

Seeking Divine Wisdom

 ## Reflection

Have you ever felt in over your head, overwhelmed, or underqualified? Solomon certainly felt that way when he became the king of Israel. He knew he was totally inadequate for the job. At the same time, he knew God is all-sufficient and would provide whatever Solomon needed to cover the occasion. When God said, "Ask for whatever you want me to give you," Solomon asked for wisdom (see 1 Kings 3:5). God was pleased with his request and graciously lavished Solomon with the gift of wisdom—as well as many other treasures.

When is the last time you asked God for wisdom? As Solomon learned, it's free for the asking! Isn't it strange how we tend to forge ahead in life without even stopping to inquire of the Lord? As humble servants of the most high God, let us not be remiss in asking him for wisdom and discernment. He is pleased with our request—and takes great joy in granting it.

Week 10

💡 My Thoughts

In what areas of my life am I "inadequate for the job"? What keeps me from asking God for wisdom and discernment?

_____

_____

_____

_____

_____

💚 My Prayer

"Omniscient and holy God, I praise you for your wisdom and love! You have created all things, and you know all things. Thank you for inviting me to ask for wisdom. Thank you for your willingness to answer that prayer. Lord, grant me wisdom as I face the challenges of today. Give me discernment as I seek to do what you have called me to do. I believe that wherever you guide me, you will provide the wisdom I need. Help me to look to you instead of depending upon my own wisdom and strength. In Jesus's name I pray, amen."

This week I am praying for: _____

_____

_____

_____

_____

_____

Seeking Divine Wisdom

 My Choices

- This week I will choose to seek God's wisdom to meet my challenges and responsibilities.

- This week I will choose to ask God for discernment in the decisions I make.

- This week I will choose to grow in God's wisdom by reading and studying his Word.

- This week I will choose to: _____

_____

_____

_____

_____

_____

 **For Further Reading:** 1 Kings 3; Proverbs 2; James 1:5

> True wisdom is a divine revelation.
>
> GEORGE BARLOW

It's All His

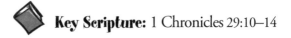 **Key Scripture:** 1 Chronicles 29:10–14

David praised the LORD in the presence of the whole assembly, saying,

> *"Praise be to you, O LORD,*
>   *God of our father Israel,*
>   *from everlasting to everlasting.*

> *Yours, O LORD, is the greatness and the power*
>   *and the glory and the majesty and the splendor,*
>   *for everything in heaven and earth is yours.*

> *Yours, O LORD is the kingdom;*
>   *you are exalted as head over all.*

> *Wealth and honor come from you;*
>   *you are the ruler of all things.*

> *In your hands are strength and power*
>   *to exalt and give strength to all.*

> *Now, our God, we give you thanks,*
>   *and praise your glorious name.*

"But who am I, and who are my people, that we should be able to give as generously as this? Everything comes from you, and we have given you only what comes from your hand."

44

It's All His

 **Reflection**

What belongs to God? Everything! Take a quiet moment right now to meditate on that truth. Everything in heaven and on earth belongs to God. Not only are wealth and material possessions his, but strength, power, and honor are his as well. God owns it all!

How should this fact affect our attitudes and actions? When we recognize that everything belongs to God, we aren't quite as possessive with material things. We take good care of the Lord's possessions, but we don't cling to them as our own. When we acknowledge that honor and power come from God, we don't get puffed up with pride; we choose thankfulness and humility instead. Knowing God owns everything changes how we give, how we react, and how we relate to God and others.

Let's turn our eyes upward in gratitude and release the tight grip we have on the "stuff" in our lives. More importantly, let's live with a sense of awe and praise for the God of all creation who holds us in his hands.

Week 11

💡 My Thoughts

Do I cling too tightly to certain things in my life? Is there something I need to release to God, knowing that it is his anyway? _____

_____

_____

_____

_____

_____

💛 My Prayer

"God of all creation, I praise you! You are the high king of heaven. Everything in heaven and on earth belongs to you. Thank you for those things you have allowed me to tend to here on earth. Thank you for the material possessions, the responsibilities, the honor, and the strength you have given me. Lord, I know it all belongs to you. Help me to keep my eyes on you and to trust you to provide everything I need. Help me to find my security in you. In Jesus's name I pray, amen."

This week I am praying for: _____

_____

_____

_____

_____

_____

My Choices

- This week I will choose to reread David's prayer in 1 Chronicles 29:10–14 every day.

- This week I will choose to look at everything in my life from the perspective of God's ownership.

- This week I will choose to thank God for the honor and power he has given me.

- This week I will choose to: _____

_____

_____

_____

_____

_____

 **For Further Reading:** 1 Chronicles 29

> All nature, including the nature of man, is a wondrous instrument of many strings, delicately tuned to work God's will and upon which he plays with a master hand.
>
> J. GRESHAM MACHEN

God's Gracious Hand

 **Key Scripture:** Ezra 7:8–10

Ezra arrived in Jerusalem in the fifth month of the seventh year of the king. He had begun his journey from Babylon on the first day of the first month, and he arrived in Jerusalem on the first day of the fifth month, for the gracious hand of his God was on him. For Ezra had devoted himself to the study and observance of the Law of the LORD, and to teaching its decrees and laws in Israel.

The Bible is alive, it speaks to me; it has feet, it runs after me; it has hands, it lays hold on me.

MARTIN LUTHER

God's Gracious Hand

 **Reflection**

"The gracious hand of his God was on him." Isn't that a beautiful picture of God's care and protection? This endearing phrase is stated three times in this chapter in reference to Ezra. Why Ezra? Why was he blessed by the presence of God's gracious hand? Surely our answer comes in the next statement, "For Ezra had devoted himself to the study and observance of the Law of the LORD." Ezra was not only a student of God's Word; he was also a doer of the Word in his daily life. He didn't live a reckless life of disobedience. Quite the contrary, he walked in God's ways and remained in his will. As a result, he was greatly blessed.

I'm not implying that if we read God's Word and walk in his ways, our lives are guaranteed to be a bed of roses. But if we follow God and obey his Word, we *will* find "rest in the shadow of the Almighty" (Psalm 91:1). We may experience difficult circumstances, but God will be with us, and his hand of protection will be upon us. May we be inspired by Ezra's passion for God's Word and his powerful example of godly living!

💡 My Thoughts

What can I do to devote myself more fully to studying and living out God's Word on a daily basis?_____

_____

_____

_____

_____

_____

💗 My Prayer

"Gracious Lord, I praise you, because you have all authority over heaven and earth. You are my sun and my shield. Thank you for watching over my life and caring for me. Help me to desire you above all else. Thank you for the beauty and power of your living Word, the Bible. Grant me the discipline to study your Word and the wisdom to live it out each day. In Jesus's name I pray, amen."

This week I am praying for: _____

_____

_____

_____

_____

_____

God's Gracious Hand

 My Choices

- This week I will choose to develop a passion for God's Word by reading it and studying it regularly.

- This week I will choose to walk in obedience to God.

- This week I will choose to thank God for his gracious hand of protection upon me.

- This week I will choose to: _____

_____

_____

_____

_____

_____

 **For Further Reading:** Psalm 119

> When you have read the Bible, you will know it is the Word of God, because you will have found it the key to your own heart, your own happiness and your own duty.
>
> WOODROW WILSON

Handling Opposition

 Key Scripture: Nehemiah 4:1–2, 4–6

When Sanballat heard that we were rebuilding the wall, he became angry and was greatly incensed. He ridiculed the Jews, and in the presence of his associates and the army of Samaria, he said, "What are those feeble Jews doing? Will they restore their wall? Will they offer sacrifices? Will they finish in a day? Can they bring the stones back to life from those heaps of rubble—burned as they are?" . . .

Hear us, O our God, for we are despised. Turn their insults back on their own heads. Give them over as plunder in a land of captivity. Do not cover up their guilt or blot out their sins from your sight, for they have thrown insults in the face of the builders.

So we rebuilt the wall till all of it reached half its height, for the people worked with all their heart.

I t is my belief that talent is plentiful, and that what is lacking is staying power.

Doris Lessing

Handling Opposition

 **Reflection**

How do you handle opposition or ridicule? Personally, my tendency is to get frustrated and want to quit or cave in to fear. Not Nehemiah! In his pursuit to rebuild the wall around Jerusalem, he prayed faithfully, worked diligently, and persevered courageously, despite significant challenges. Time and time again throughout the book of Nehemiah, we see him taking his concerns to the Lord with a contrite heart, not a complaining spirit.

What a tremendous example for us as we face challenges in our lives! Whether we experience a small frustration during the day or a major life disappointment, we can learn from the way Nehemiah handled his setbacks. We, too, can seek the Lord's direction and help, work with diligence, and persevere with courage. When challenges come, and they will, we do not need to fret. Nehemiah was tough—and with God's strength, we can be too.

Week 13

💡 My Thoughts

What opposition or challenge am I facing in my life right now? How can I be like Nehemiah in the way I handle it?

_____

_____

_____

_____

_____

♡ My Prayer

"Great and powerful God, I praise you, because you know all things and can do all things. Thank you for giving me the courage and strength to make it through the opposition and challenges I face in my life. Thank you for your promise that you will never leave me. When things get tough, you are right there beside me. Help me to be faithful to do the work you have set before me. Give me the wisdom and guidance to persevere with diligence. In Jesus's name I pray, amen."

This week I am praying for: _____

_____

_____

_____

_____

_____

_____

Handling Opposition

 My Choices

- This week I will choose to seek the Lord's strength and guidance when I face a challenge.

- This week I will choose to persevere with courage and work with diligence even when the going gets tough.

- This week I will choose to be an encourager to others, not a discourager.

- This week I will choose to: _____

_____

_____

_____

_____

_____

 For Further Reading: Nehemiah 1–4

> Our greatest weakness lies in giving up. The most certain way to succeed is always to try just one more time.
>
> THOMAS ALVA EDISON

Respectable Requests

Key Scripture: Esther 7:1–4

So the king and Haman went to dine with Queen Esther, and as they were drinking wine on that second day, the king again asked, "Queen Esther, what is your petition? It will be given you. What is your request? Even up to half the kingdom, it will be granted."

Then Queen Esther answered, "If I have found favor with you, O king, and if it pleases your majesty, grant me my life—this is my petition. And spare my people—this is my request. For I and my people have been sold for destruction and slaughter and annihilation. If we had merely been sold as male and female slaves I would have kept quiet, because no such distress would justify disturbing the king."

Diplomacy: The art of jumping into troubled waters without making a splash.

ART LINKLETTER

Respectable Requests

 **Reflection**

Humbly, carefully, wisely, Esther made her request known to the king. She wasn't speaking off the cuff. On the contrary, a few days before she had encouraged her people to begin to pray. Then she had invited the king and his right-hand man to dinner two nights in a row. On the first night, the king asked her what she wanted. If I had been in Esther's place, I would have blabbed my request right then and there. But Esther knew better than to nag or blab or push. With great patience and restraint, she simply invited the king and his assistant to a second dinner. It was during the second dinner she submitted her request—which the king gladly granted.

How do you typically go about presenting a request to someone? For many of us, nagging, complaining, whining, and gossiping are standard procedure. We could all take a lesson from Esther's example. First, take the request to the Lord, seeking his help and guidance. Next, use patience and wisdom to determine the right time and place to share the request. Finally, respectfully submit the request, knowing it has been prayerfully considered and thoroughly thought through.

The king listened to Esther, granted her request, and saved her and her people. What can God do through us as we submit our requests in the same patient, thoughtful, and respectful way?

Week 14

💡 My Thoughts

How do I need to change the way I ask or submit requests to my family members, my friends, my coworkers, and others?

_____

_____

_____

_____

_____

💗 My Prayer

"Sovereign and holy God, I praise you for the powerful work you are doing in my life. Thank you that even though you are the high king of heaven, you still bend your ear to hear my requests. How amazing! Lord, help me to be wise. Forgive me for all the times I've resorted to nagging, whining, or pushing to get what I want. Give me patience, grace, and humility as I submit my petitions and requests to others. In Jesus's name I pray, amen."

This week I am praying for: _____

_____

_____

_____

_____

_____

_____

Respectable Requests

 My Choices

- This week I will choose to prayerfully consider the requests I plan to make of others.

- This week I will choose to use wisdom and discretion when making a request.

- This week I will choose to submit all petitions and requests with wisdom, humility, and respect.

- This week I will choose to: _____

_____

_____

_____

_____

_____

 **For Further Reading:** The book of Esther

> You never know till you try to reach them how accessible men are: but you must approach each man by the right door.
>
> HENRY WARD BEECHER

Trust beyond Understanding

 **Key Scripture:** Job 42:1–5

Then Job replied to the LORD:

"I know that you can do all things;
no plan of yours can be thwarted.
You asked, 'Who is this that
obscures my counsel without knowledge?'
Surely I spoke of things I did not understand,
things too wonderful for me to know.

You said, 'Listen now, and I will speak;
I will question you,
and you shall answer me.'
My ears had heard of you
but now my eyes have seen you."

If one thing lies at the basis of the whole biblical teaching about God, it is that God knows all things.

J. GRESHAM MACHEN

Trust beyond Understanding

 ## Reflection

Job had been acquainted with God when his life was moving along smoothly, but he truly got to know, love, and respect God through the struggles and challenges he faced. He saw God is bigger than we can ever imagine. He realized God is God, and we are not. God can be trusted, but he can't be understood. His ways are far above us; we only have a small understanding of the scope of his wisdom and power.

Have you ever wrestled with the "whys" of life? Job did, and God's answer to Job was simple: as limited human beings, we are unable to completely understand God's ways. Dear friend, are you going through a time of challenge, or perhaps suffering? Are you willing to fall into the arms of your loving heavenly Father and trust him to help you through? We may never understand why a certain thing happens, but we can trust our loving God. He is with us through the difficulties and the pain.

Week 15

💡 My Thoughts

Am I willing to trust God through my struggles, even if I
don't understand the reasons or can't answer the "whys"?

_____

_____

_____

_____

_____

_____

♡ My Prayer

"Glorious and awesome God, you are too wonderful! I
adore you. I praise you, for you know all things. Your ways
are high above mine, and your thoughts are beyond mine.
I trust your loving hand. Thank you for being my Good
Shepherd. Thank you for taking care of me when I don't
know what to do or which way to turn. Thank you for never
leaving me. Grant me strength for today, and help me to rest
in your loving arms. In Jesus's name I pray, amen."

This week I am praying for: _____

_____

_____

_____

_____

_____

Trust beyond Understanding

 My Choices

- This week I will choose to trust God through the difficulties in my life.

- This week I will choose to seek God and grow to know him better through the struggles as well as the smooth times.

- This week I will choose to place my hope in God instead of wallowing in self-pity.

- This week I will choose to: _____

_____

_____

_____

_____

_____

 **For Further Reading:** Job 38–41

> A man's concept of God creates
> his attitude toward
> the hour in which he lives.
>
> G. CAMPBELL MORGAN

Radiant Faith

 **Key Scripture:** Psalm 34:4–8

I sought the LORD, and he answered me;
he delivered me from all my fears.
Those who look to him are radiant;
their faces are never covered with shame.
This poor man called, and the LORD
heard him;
he saved him out of all his troubles.
The angel of the LORD encamps around
those who fear him,
and he delivers them.

Taste and see that the LORD is good;
blessed is the man who takes refuge
in him.

I know not the way he leads me, but well do I know my Guide. What have I to fear?

MARTIN LUTHER

Radiant Faith

 **Reflection**

When fear comes knocking at your door, how do you answer? It's so easy for us to open the door and allow fear to come in—fear of failure, fear of something harmful happening to our kids, fear of financial loss, fear of abandonment. When we give in to fear, it quickly overtakes our hearts and minds. It consumes us and discourages us.

But we don't have to give in; we can yield to God instead. Our passage today reminds us of the awesome blessing and strength that comes from giving our fears to the Lord and finding our refuge in him. The psalmist didn't say he was without fear; rather, he openly declared that he sought the Lord, and God delivered him from his fears.

When fear is at the door, seek God. Call out to him. Remember, the angel of the Lord is encamped around us to deliver us. Our faith will be strengthened as we taste the goodness of the Lord and find our safety and security in him. May our faces be radiant with the beauty that comes from walking in faith, not fear!

Week 16

💡 My Thoughts

What fears have I allowed to come into my life? Am I willing to seek the Lord and ask him to replace my fears with faith?

_____

_____

_____

_____

_____

_____

💗 My Prayer

"Great and mighty God, you are my rock and my refuge. I praise you for being my ever-present help in time of need. May I never lose sight of your protection and provision. Thank you for hearing my prayers. Please take away my fears, and replace them with faith. Help me to give my worries, fears, and cares to you day by day. Grant me the true security that only comes from a relationship with you. In Jesus's name I pray, amen."

This week I am praying for: _____

_____

_____

_____

_____

_____

My Choices

- This week I will choose to seek the Lord and give my fears to him.

- This week I will choose to remember that God is always with me.

- This week I will choose to look to the Lord for my security and strength, and I will be radiant with faith in him.

- This week I will choose to: _____

_____

_____

_____

_____

_____

 **For Further Reading:** Psalms 33–35

> A Christian's despair makes him pray;
> it is a despair of self. A worlding's
> despair makes him rave against
> God and give up prayer.
>
> CHARLES H. SPURGEON

Positive Principles for Life

 **Key Scripture:** Proverbs 3:3–8

Let love and faithfulness never leave you;
bind them around your neck,
write them on the tablet of your heart.
Then you will win favor and a good name
in the sight of God and man.
Trust in the LORD with all your heart
and lean not on your own understanding;
in all your ways acknowledge him,
and he will make your paths straight.

Do not be wise in your own eyes;
fear the LORD and shun evil.
This will bring health to your body and
nourishment to your bones.

There is no conceivable situation in which it is not safe to trust God.

J. OSWALD SANDERS

Positive Principles for Life

 **Reflection**

The book of Proverbs is overflowing with positive principles for life. Here, in a few short verses, we receive a power-packed message. Be loving and loyal. Trust God and acknowledge him in everything. Don't be prideful; instead, fear God and shun evil. Generally speaking, living according to these principles will lead us to the wonderful rewards of good health and a good name in the sight of God and man.

The central focus of this passage is the instruction to "trust the LORD with all your heart." How do we develop wholehearted trust? We begin by believing God is who he says he is—the sovereign, holy, all-powerful Creator of the universe. We refuse to trust ourselves or our own wisdom; we refuse to become arrogant in any way. Instead of focusing on what we can't do, we focus on what God *can* do. This week let's turn our hearts toward trusting God fully. Let's examine our lives and humbly seek his ways. When we make the choice to trust God wholeheartedly—*that's* when we begin to experience life to the fullest!

Week 17

💡 My Thoughts

Am I seeking God for wisdom to live my life and trusting him with all my heart? What can I do to develop wholehearted trust? _____

_____

_____

_____

_____

_____

💗 My Prayer

"God of all wisdom, I praise you, because you know all things and can do all things. Thank you for being trustworthy. Lead me and strengthen my faith. Help me to acknowledge you in all my ways. Bring glory to yourself through my life as I humbly walk in faith, trusting you with my whole heart. In Jesus's name I pray, amen."

This week I am praying for: _____

_____

_____

_____

_____

_____

Positive Principles for Life

 My Choices

- This week I will choose to be filled with love and faithfulness toward others.

- This week I will choose to trust the Lord with all my heart.

- This week I will choose to turn from self-centeredness and pride and instead acknowledge God in all my ways.

- This week I will choose to: _____

_____

_____

_____

_____

_____

 **For Further Reading:** Proverbs 2–4

> None are so empty as those
> who are full of themselves.
>
> BENJAMIN WHICHCOTE

The Power of Friendship

 **Key Scripture:** Ecclesiastes 4:9–12

Two are better than one,
because they have a good return
for their work:
If one falls down,
his friend can help him up.
But pity the man who falls
and has no one to help him up!
Also, if two lie down together, they will
keep warm.
But how can one keep warm alone?
Though one may be overpowered,
two can defend themselves.
A cord of three strands is not quickly broken.

Be slow to fall into friendship, but when thou art in, continue firm and constant.

SOCRATES

The Power of Friendship

 **Reflection**

It's easy to become independent and go our own way, isn't it? In a culture that glorifies self-reliance, we often lose sight of our need for one another. But no man is an island unto himself. God created us to interact with others and to work together. In Proverbs 27:17 Solomon said, "As iron sharpens iron, so one man sharpens another." Strength, encouragement, admonishment, and growth are the results of true friendship. We need our friends!

As in any area of life, though, we must keep a healthy balance. We must acknowledge our need for friends but not become overdependent upon other people. There are no perfect friends who can meet all our needs. Christ himself is the only perfect friend. Let us recognize the blessing that comes from having healthy friendships and be deliberate about building and maintaining those bonds. Most of all, let's work to build and maintain the bonds of friendship with Jesus.

Week 18

💡 My Thoughts

Do I have friendships that provide strength, encouragement, admonishment, and growth in my life? Am I there for my friends when they need me? _____

_____

_____

_____

_____

_____

💙 My Prayer

"Gracious and loving Father, I praise you, because you are the perfect friend. I praise you for the perfect love you have toward me. Thank you for forgiving my sins. Help me to forgive others. Thank you for the compassion and mercy you show toward me, and help me to reflect compassion and mercy toward others. Give me wisdom to reach out and build new friendships, and help me to be a good friend. In Jesus's name I pray, amen."

This week I am praying for: _____

_____

_____

_____

_____

_____

The Power of Friendship

 My Choices

- This week I will choose to be an encouragement and strength to my friends.

- This week I will choose to pray for my friends each day.

- This week I will choose to be open to new friendships God may want to bring into my life.

- This week I will choose to: _____

_____

_____

_____

_____

 **For Further Reading:** Ecclesiastes 3–5

> Look around today and share a
> cheerful, friendly smile;
> Show the world you truly care,
> then go the second mile.
>
> WILLIAM A. WARD

The Gift of Affirmation

 **Key Scripture:** Song of Solomon 2:3–6

Beloved
> Like an apple tree among the trees of the forest
>   is my lover among the young men.
> I delight to sit in his shade,
>   and his fruit is sweet to my taste.
> He has taken me to the banquet hall,
>   and his banner over me is love.
> Strengthen me with raisins,
>   refresh me with apples,
>   for I am faint with love.
> His left arm is under my head,
>   and his right arm embraces me.

Words are . . . the most powerful drug
used by mankind.

RUDYARD KIPLING

The Gift of Affirmation

 Reflection

The words of "the beloved" reflect her great love and admiration for her lover. The entire Song of Solomon is filled with a beautiful banter of lovingly uplifting words between two people who care deeply for one another. As I read these verses, I can't help but wonder: what do the people who are nearest and dearest to our hearts hear from us? Is it mostly beautiful words of encouragement and affirmation? Or is it mostly nagging, complaining, orders, and demands?

Think about the effect the words of the beloved had on her lover. They built him up. They nurtured and strengthened the relationship they enjoyed together. Uplifting words have a positive effect on our relationships with others, yet we rarely realize their power. Our tongues can be a delightful source of encouragement or a dreadful source of discouragement. May we graciously and cautiously use our words for God's glory and others' blessing!

💡 My Thoughts

Am I using my words to bless others, or do I use them to
bring people down? _____

_____

_____

_____

_____

💗 My Prayer

"Holy and wise God, I praise you, because you are kind
and good. Your words are faithful and true. Thank you for
being gentle and gracious with me. Help me to be gracious
and kind with my words, especially when I speak to the
people who are closest to me. Please help me see the best in
my family and friends. May that admiration spill over into
kind and encouraging words to them! Give me the joy of
knowing I have lifted up those I love through the power of
my words. In Jesus's name I pray, amen."

This week I am praying for: _____

_____

_____

_____

_____

_____

The Gift of Affirmation

 **My Choices**

- This week I will choose to use words of admiration and encouragement in speaking to those I love.

- This week I will choose to guard my tongue from speaking words of empty flattery or deceit.

- This week I will choose to turn from nagging and complaining and only speak words that lift others up.

- This week I will choose to: _____

_____

_____

_____

_____

_____

For Further Reading: Song of Solomon 1–2

People have a way of becoming
what you encourage them to be—
not what you nag them to be.

SCUDDER N. PARKER

We Are His

 **Key Scripture:** Isaiah 64:8–9

Yet, O LORD, you are our Father.
We are the clay, you are the potter;
we are all the work of your hand.
Do not be angry beyond measure, O LORD;
do not remember our sins forever.
Oh, look upon us, we pray,
for we are all your people.

We should never tire of the thought of God's power.

DONALD GREY BARNHOUSE

 **Reflection**

How do you view your relationship with God? Do you recognize God as a loving Father to you? No matter what kind of relationship we've had with our earthly fathers, we can rest assured our heavenly Father loves us abundantly and cares for us completely. He is our molder and our maker. Just as a potter gently forms a lump of clay into a beautiful and useful vessel, so our loving heavenly Father gently forms and fashions us for a purpose.

Dear friend, don't be dismayed or discouraged by your mistakes or weaknesses. You are not a finished product. God is continuing to make you into a lovely and usable vessel specifically designed for his glory. Don't let setbacks or U-turns get you down; look instead to your wonderful Creator, and seek his loving help and direction. May each of us be moldable, teachable, and flexible, knowing that God is preparing us for a specific plan. He is our careful and gentle potter. Let's be pliable in his hands!

Week 20

💡 My Thoughts

In what ways do I see God gently molding and making me for a purpose? _____

_____

_____

_____

_____

_____

♡ My Prayer

"Holy and gracious heavenly Father, I praise you for your great power and love. You are the perfect Father. Thank you for the plan and purpose you have for my life. Thank you for continuing to mold me and make me for that purpose. I confess there are times when I harden my heart or don't listen to you. Help me to be teachable and flexible. Smooth over my rough edges, and work around my weaknesses. Make me into a vessel that glorifies you. In Jesus's name I pray, amen."

This week I am praying for: _____

_____

_____

_____

_____

We Are His

 My Choices

- This week I will choose to see God as my loving heavenly Father.

- This week I will choose to seek God's strength and wisdom when I experience setbacks or make mistakes.

- This week I will choose to trust that God has a plan and purpose for my life.

- This week I will choose to: _____

_____

_____

_____

_____

 **For Further Reading:** Isaiah 55–56

> When a train goes through a tunnel
> and it gets dark, you don't throw
> away the ticket and jump off. You
> sit still and trust the engineer.
>
> CORRIE TEN BOOM

Big Plans

 **Key Scripture:** Jeremiah 1:4–9

The word of the LORD came to me, saying,

> *"Before I formed you in the womb I knew you,*
> *before you were born I set you apart;*
> *I appointed you as a prophet to the nations."*

"Ah, Sovereign LORD," I said, "I do not know how to speak; I am only a child."

But the LORD said to me, "Do not say, 'I am only a child.' You must go to everyone I send you to and say whatever I command you. Do not be afraid of them, for I am with you and will rescue you," declares the LORD.

Then the LORD reached out his hand and touched my mouth and said to me, "Now, I have put my words in your mouth."

There is no thrill quite like doing something you didn't know you could.

MARJORIE HOLMES

Big Plans

Reflection

Where God guides, he provides! Certainly we see this in the life of Jeremiah, and we can expect to see it in our lives too. Jeremiah was appointed before he was even born. Isn't that amazing? As Jeremiah was being formed in his mother's womb, God was equipping him and setting him apart for a special purpose. God makes no mistakes. God gave Jeremiah the skills he needed in order to do what he was called to do.

Imagine! God had a plan for you even before you were born. He formed you exactly according to his plan, and he has equipped you with everything you need to fulfill your calling. Do you believe this truth? Do you trust that God has equipped you and will continue to equip you for the plans he has for you? Are you willing to give up your fear of inadequacy? Just as God spoke to Jeremiah, he is also saying to you and me, "Don't be afraid, for I am with you."

My Thoughts

What fears of inadequacy do I need to give over to God?

_____

_____

_____

_____

_____

_____

My Prayer

"Glorious Father, I praise you, because you are all-knowing and all-powerful. You formed me in my mother's womb, and you made me for a unique purpose. Thank you for equipping me for the tasks you have prepared for me to do. Thank you for being with me and never leaving me. Help me to follow you as I move forward in faith. Please give me strength for the journey you have set before me. In Jesus's name I pray, amen."

This week I am praying for: _____

_____

_____

_____

_____

Big Plans

 My Choices

- This week I will choose to recognize that God has had a plan for my life since before I was born.

- This week I will choose to trust him to equip me for what he has called me to do.

- This week I will choose to thank God for being with me and rescuing me when I'm in trouble.

- This week I will choose to: _____

_____

_____

_____

_____

_____

 **For Further Reading:** Jeremiah 29–31

> All God's giants have been weak men and women who did great things for God because they believed that God would be with them.
>
> J. Hudson Taylor

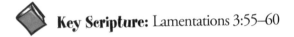

Week 22

He Is Near

Key Scripture: Lamentations 3:55–60

I called on your name, O LORD,
from the depths of the pit.
You heard my plea; "Do not close your ears
to my cry for relief."
You came near when I called you,
and you said, "Do not fear."
O Lord, you took up my case;
you redeemed my life.
You have seen, O LORD, the wrong done to me.
Uphold my cause!
You have seen the depth of their vengeance,
all their plots against me.

We must shed tears if we would hereafter
have them wiped away.

RICHARD SIBBES

He Is Near

 **Reflection**

"The depths of the pit." Been there? Whether we're going through life-altering events or temporary challenges, there are times in life when we feel as if we're in "the pits." Jeremiah certainly felt that way. As a prophet of the Lord, he faced significant challenges and heavy persecution. His example demonstrates that serving the Lord offers no guarantee of an easy life. But like Jeremiah, we can rest assured of one truth: no matter how difficult our journey is, God will never leave us. Our loving and powerful God is with us.

Jeremiah cried out to God from the pit, and God came near. God comforted Jeremiah and told him not to fear. When we find ourselves in the pit, let's remember to look up, cry out to God, and feel his loving arms around us. After all, God sees everything that happens to us, and he will take up our cause.

Week 22

💡 My Thoughts

How do I handle "the pits" in life? Do I cry out to God, or do I simply whine and complain? _____

_____

_____

_____

_____

_____

💜 My Prayer

"Marvelous and awesome God, I praise you, because you are the God who sees all things. You know when I am struggling. You know the challenges I face—even the ones I can't see yet. You know the enemy's plans against me and the hurts I've experienced at the hands of others. Thank you for taking up my case and redeeming my life from the pit. Thank you for hearing my plea and watching over me. Help me not to fear but rather to trust you through the challenges of my life. In Jesus's name I pray, amen."

This week I am praying for: _____

_____

_____

_____

_____

_____

He Is Near

 **My Choices**

- This week I will choose to call on the name of the Lord when I face troubles or challenges.
- This week I will choose to remember that God hears my voice, and he is near.
- This week I will choose to allow God to take up my case against my enemies.
- This week I will choose to: _____

_____

_____

_____

_____

_____

 **For Further Reading:** Psalms 115–117

> The best style of prayer is that
> which cannot be called
> anything else but a cry.
>
> CHARLES H. SPURGEON

Tough Assignment

 **Key Scripture:** Ezekiel 2:3–5

He [God] said: "Son of man, I am sending you to the Israelites, to a rebellious nation that has rebelled against me; they and their fathers have been in revolt against me to this very day. The people to whom I am sending you are obstinate and stubborn. Say to them, 'This is what the Sovereign LORD says.' And whether they listen or fail to listen—for they are a rebellious house—they will know that a prophet has been among them."

No one would ever have crossed the ocean if he could have gotten off the ship in the storm.

CHARLES F. KETTERING

Tough Assignment

 **Reflection**

Not quite the cushy job we would sign up for, right? In this passage, God called Ezekiel to bring his message to an obstinate and stubborn audience—a group of rebellious people who were predisposed not to even listen to him. As Ezekiel learned, God doesn't always call us to happy jobs and fun assignments. Sometimes the tasks he puts before us are rather unpleasant, even ugly. Our inclination may be to run from such jobs. But if we run, we will certainly miss something extraordinary.

Extraordinary? Absolutely! When God calls us to a new task that stretches and challenges us—whether it's on a mission field in India, in the business world in Dallas, or at a home in Peoria—he is asking us to step out of the easy and into the extraordinary. He is placing us in a position where we must look to him and say, "Only by your grace and strength can I do this." Trusting God in the uneasy situations of life is an opportunity for us to grow in faith as we watch his mighty hand at work.

Week 23

💡 My Thoughts

What does God want to teach me through the not-so-pleasant assignments in my life? _____

_____

_____

_____

_____

_____

💗 My Prayer

"Wonderful, loving God, I praise you, because you have all power and all authority. When you call me to a new task, no matter how difficult, I know I can trust you. You see the whole picture, while I only see in part. Thank you for being my strength in difficult situations. Open my eyes to see your hand at work when things get tough. Give me encouragement, and help me persevere through every task you put before me. Be close to me during the easy times, and help me feel your loving arms around me during the difficult times. In Jesus's name I pray, amen."

This week I am praying for: _____

_____

_____

_____

_____

Tough Assignment

 My Choices

- This week I will choose to accept the fact that God may call me to jobs that are not pretty or easy.

- This week I will choose to persevere through the challenges of life with God's strength.

- This week I will choose to trust God in the difficult situations as well as the pleasant ones.

- This week I will choose to: _____

_____

_____

_____

_____

_____

 **For Further Reading:** Ezekiel 33–34

> Never measure the height of
> a mountain until you
> have reached the top. Then
> you will see how low it was.
>
> Dag Hammarskjold

Week 24

Handwriting on the Wall

 **Key Scripture:** Daniel 5:17, 22–24

Then Daniel answered the king . . .

"But you his son, O Belshazzar, have not humbled yourself, though you knew all this. Instead, you have set yourself up against the Lord of heaven. You had the goblets from his temple brought to you, and you and your nobles, your wives and your concubines drank wine from them. You praised the gods of silver and gold, of bronze, iron, wood and stone, which cannot see or hear or understand. But you did not honor the God who holds in his hand your life and all your ways. Therefore he sent the hand that wrote the inscription."

The cure for boasting is to boast in the Lord all the day long.

CHARLES H. SPURGEON

96

Handwriting on the Wall

 **Reflection**

King Belshazzar's extravagant party was interrupted by a disturbing and unusual sight. The fingers of a human hand appeared out of thin air and wrote on the wall plaster. Now, you don't see that every day! God was giving a clear message to the arrogant king, letting him know judgment would soon be coming. And in fact, that very night Belshazzar's kingdom was attacked and taken from him. Today the phrase "handwriting on the wall" is commonly used to refer to impending doom or misfortune.

We don't need to see the handwriting on the wall to know what God requires of us, because he has given us his Word. Are we paying attention to how he wants us to live? King Belshazzar chose to ignore the sovereign God who held his life in his hand, so God used a hand to bring a message of judgment. Dear friend, let's not make the same mistake by walking in pride and ignoring God's commands. Instead, let's acknowledge God in all our ways and give him all the glory.

💡 My Thoughts

Am I ignoring God's Word in certain areas of my life? In what areas do I need to recognize pride and get rid of it?

_____

_____

_____

_____

_____

💟 My Prayer

"Sovereign and holy God, I praise you, for you are the Creator of all things and the one true God. I praise you because you are the one who holds my life in your hands. You are the one who blesses me and puts me in a place of honor. Lord, I acknowledge that it is from your hand I have received everything I have. Deliver me from pride, and help me to obey your Word. Thank you for your goodness and mercy toward me. Help me to give you all the glory all the days of my life. In Jesus's name I pray, amen."

This week I am praying for: _____

_____

_____

_____

_____

_____

Handwriting on the Wall

 My Choices

- This week I will choose to pay attention to the lessons God is teaching me through his Word.

- This week I will choose to recognize and confess areas of pride.

- This week I will choose to thank the Lord for holding my life in his hands.

- This week I will choose to: _____

_____

_____

_____

_____

_____

 **For Further Reading:** Daniel 4–6

All that I am I owe to Jesus Christ,
revealed to me in His divine Book.

DAVID LIVINGSTONE

Consequences of Sin

 **Key Scripture:** Hosea 4:1–3; 14:1

Hear the word of the LORD, you Israelites,
because the LORD has a charge to bring
against you who live in the land:
"There is no faithfulness, no love,
no acknowledgement of God in the land.
There is only cursing, lying and murder,
stealing and adultery;
they break all bounds,
and bloodshed follows bloodshed.
Because of this the land mourns,
and all who live in it waste away;
the beasts of the field and the birds of the air
and the fish of the sea are dying." . . .

Return, O Israel, to the LORD your God.
Your sins have been your downfall!

Sin is the greatest robber that this world will ever know.

PETER CLEMENT

Consequences of Sin

 **Reflection**

Sin is ugly. Generally speaking, sinful lifestyles result in serious, negative consequences. Sin brings destruction and pain, not only to those who choose to go against God's commands, but often to those around them too.

The Lord tells his people to be holy, set apart. He tells us to live righteous lives—not out of cruelty to make our lives miserable, but rather out of love to make our lives wonderful. God wants us to experience the joy and blessing of lives lived in integrity and righteousness. Make no mistake, our wonderful Lord is a forgiving God; but that doesn't mean he takes away the awful consequences—to ourselves and to others—when we choose to sin.

In our passage today we see Hosea warning God's people about the consequences of sin. But he also encouraged them to repent, for the Lord's desire is to redeem lives. As Proverbs 14:34 says, "Righteousness exalts a nation, but sin is a disgrace to any people." Sinful lifestyles ravage and tear apart a culture. Righteous lifestyles turn that tide. May you and I stand for righteousness in our time!

💡 My Thoughts

Is there an area of sin in my life for which I need to repent?

_____

_____

_____

_____

_____

_____

💗 My Prayer

"Holy and perfect God, I praise you, for you are good. I praise you, because you are loving and kind. I confess I often ignore your ways and turn to my own ways. Thank you for forgiving me. Lead me away from temptation, and deliver me from evil. Help me to desire righteousness, and give me grace to walk in your ways each day. Help me recognize sin and turn from it. Give me strength to live a life of righteousness and integrity. In Jesus's name I pray, amen."

This week I am praying for: _____

_____

_____

_____

_____

_____

Consequences of Sin

 ## My Choices

- This week I will choose to ask the Lord to reveal and convict me of sin in my life.

- This week I will choose to seek his help and strength in turning from sin.

- This week I will choose to thank the Lord for his redeeming love.

- This week I will choose to: _____

_____

_____

_____

_____

_____

 **For Further Reading:** Hosea 13–14

> It is the tendency of righteousness
> to produce blessedness, as it is the
> tendency of evil to produce misery.
>
> CHARLES HODGE

He Makes All Things New

 **Key Scripture:** Joel 2:25–27

I will repay you for the years the
locust have eaten—
the great locust and the young locust,
the other locusts and the locust swarm—
my great army that I sent among you.
You will have plenty to eat, until you are full,
and you will praise the name of the
LORD your God,
who has worked wonders for you;
never again will my people be shamed.
Then you will know that I am in Israel,
that I am the LORD your God,
and that there is no other;
never again will my people be shamed.

When you say a situation or a person is hopeless, you are slamming the door in the face of God.

CHARLES L. ALLEN

He Makes All Things New

Reflection

Have you made a bad mistake or terrible choice and feel as if nothing good will ever come of it? Or has someone else done something to you, and you think you will never recover? God's message to the Israelites is a message of hope we can receive today. The Lord our God is able to bring restoration out of the worst of circumstances. Nothing that happens in our lives is a surprise to him, and no problem is too big for him. We can turn to the Lord, our great healer, and hand him the broken pieces of our lives. He redeemed the devastated land of Israel, and he can redeem the devastation in our lives too.

Of course, the greatest redemptive act of all is the salvation we have received through Christ's sacrifice for us on the cross. Once we were ravaged with sin; now we have been made new in Christ. Truly, God makes all things new!

Week 26

💡 My Thoughts

How have I seen God's restoring power at work in my life and circumstances? _____

_____

_____

_____

_____

_____

💜 My Prayer

"Lord God Almighty, I praise you, because you are a God of redemption. You are able to do all things. You are my creator and my restorer. Thank you for taking the broken pieces of my life and putting them back together in a new way. Nothing is impossible with you! Lord, I need your help and your healing power. Please bring restoration to my life in the area of _____. I trust that you are working in ways I cannot see, and I trust your loving hands to bring redemption and renewal to my life. In Jesus's name I pray, amen."

This week I am praying for: _____

_____

_____

_____

_____

He Makes All Things New

 My Choices

- This week I will choose to look to God for hope instead of focusing on despair.

- This week I will choose to ask God to redeem the broken pieces in my life.

- This week I will choose to share this message of hope with the people around me.

- This week I will choose to: _____

_____

_____

_____

_____

_____

 **For Further Reading:** Joel 1–2

My God! how excellent thy grace,
Whence all our hope and comfort springs!
The sons of Adam in distress
Fly to the shadow of thy wings.

ISAAC WATTS

God Confidence

 **Key Scripture:** Obadiah 1–3

The vision of Obadiah.

*This is what the Sovereign LORD says
about Edom—*

We have heard a message from the LORD:
An envoy was sent to the nations to say,
"Rise, and let us go against her for battle"—
"See, I will make you small among the nations;
you will be utterly despised.
The pride of your heart has deceived you,
you who live in the clefts of the rocks
and make your home on the heights,
you who say to yourself,
'Who can bring me down to the ground?'"

Pride goes before destruction, a haughty
spirit before a fall.

SOLOMON

God Confidence

 **Reflection**

Confidence is a good thing; pride is not. The Edomites were a self-reliant people, taking pride in the safety of their rock fortress. But according to God, their pride had deceived them into thinking they were invincible. Clearly, they found their strength in themselves and not in the Lord.

Where do you find your strength and security? Do you take refuge in the Lord, or do you trust in your own strength and circumstances? When life is going well, it's easy to allow pride to seep into our hearts and place our sense of worth and security in things—a big bank account, a good job, strong health, many friends. These things in themselves aren't bad; but when they become our source of security and pride, we're walking on shaky ground. Dear friend, instead of putting our confidence in material possessions or status or people, let's live with confidence in our sovereign God. Let's recognize our need of him. He alone is our rock, our refuge, and our redeemer.

My Thoughts

Do I base my confidence and security on God or on things? Are there areas of pride and self-righteousness in my life that need to change? _____

_____

_____

_____

_____

_____

My Prayer

"All-sufficient God, I praise you for your mighty power and strength. You are my rock and my refuge, my very present help in time of need. I recognize all I have comes from you. Thank you for watching over me and protecting me. Examine my heart and alert me to pride. Help me to live my life with God-confidence instead of self-confidence. In Jesus's name I pray, amen."

This week I am praying for: _____

_____

_____

_____

_____

_____

God Confidence

 My Choices

- This week I will choose to live confidently with my eyes on God.

- This week I will choose to recognize that my security comes from God, not from things or circumstances.

- This week I will choose to acknowledge God as the almighty and sovereign Lord of my life.

- This week I will choose to: _____

_____

_____

_____

_____

_____

 **For Further Reading:** Psalms 71–73

> Success can go to my head, and it
> will, unless I remember that it is
> God who accomplishes the work.
>
> CHARLES H. SPURGEON

Prayer from the Fish's Belly

 **Key Scripture:** Jonah 2:1–6

From inside the fish Jonah prayed to the LORD his God. He said:

> *"In my distress I called to the LORD,*
> *and he answered me.*
> *From the depths of the grave I called for help,*
> *and you listened to my cry.*
> *You hurled me into the deep,*
> *into the very heart of the seas,*
> *and the currents swirled about me;*
> *all your waves and breakers swept over me.*
> *I said, 'I have been banished*
> *from your sight;*
> *yet I will look again*
> *toward your holy temple.'*
> *Then engulfing waters threatened me,*
> *the deep surrounded me;*
> *seaweed was wrapped around my head.*
> *To the roots of the mountains I sank down;*
> *the earth beneath barred me in forever.*
> *But you brought my life up from the pit,*
> *O LORD my God."*

Prayer from the Fish's Belly

 Reflection

Can't you just picture Jonah sitting there in the dark, slimy belly of the fish, with seaweed wrapped around his head? He was at the lowest of the low. Life couldn't get any worse. Jonah must have been thinking to himself, *How did I get myself into such a fix? Will God still hear my cry from this dark place?*

Perhaps you've had those same thoughts a time or two. The good news is, no matter how low we go, no matter how deep and dark the pit we create for ourselves, we can still cry out to God. He is still with us. We can't flee from his presence, and we can't move away from his love. No matter what we have done, no matter where we find ourselves, we can still call on him, and he will hear us. Isn't it wonderful to know we are never out of God's hearing range—or his arm's reach?

Week 28

💡 My Thoughts

When do I feel most alone? In those times, do I cry out to God, or do I fret and despair?_____

_____

_____

_____

_____

_____

💗 My Prayer

"Marvelous, powerful, and loving God, I praise you, because you are always with me. I cannot flee from your presence. Thank you for staying close and hearing my prayer. Thank you for loving me even when I've tried to run the other way. Help me to keep my eyes on you and to cry out to you when I feel like wallowing in regret or despair. Thank you for your wonderful, ever-present love. In Jesus's name I pray, amen."

This week I am praying for: _____

_____

_____

_____

_____

_____

Prayer from the Fish's Belly

 My Choices

- This week I will choose to cry out to God, no matter how dark my circumstances.

- This week I will choose to thank God for his constant presence in my life.

- This week I will choose to walk in obedience to Christ.

- This week I will choose to: _____

_____

_____

_____

_____

_____

 **For Further Reading:** Psalms 103 and 139

> The notion that there is a God but that he is comfortably far away is not embodied in the doctrinal statement of any Christian church.
>
> A. W. TOZER

Fearsome but Loving

 **Key Scripture:** Nahum 1:3, 6–8

The LORD is slow to anger and great in power;
the LORD will not leave the guilty unpunished.
His way is in the whirlwind and the storm,
and clouds are the dust of his feet. . . .
Who can withstand his indignation?
Who can endure his fierce anger?
His wrath is poured out like fire;
the rocks are shattered before him.
The LORD is good, a refuge in times of trouble.
He cares for those who trust in him,
but with an overwhelming flood
he will make an end of Nineveh;
he will pursue his foes into darkness.

There is terror in the Bible as well as comfort.

DONALD GREY BARNHOUSE

Fearsome but Loving

 **Reflection**

The little book of Nahum gives us a morsel of insight into the magnificent mystery of God. We see the portrait of both a patient God and a God to be feared. He is holy and just, yet loving and merciful. Perhaps you have met people who say they only believe in a "loving God," not one who would ever punish or judge. Yet, if we are going to follow God, we must look at the whole picture of who he says he is, not just the safe, happy parts.

The beauty of the whole picture is that we serve an all-powerful God. He shows vengeance and wrath, yet he is slow to anger and filled with loving-kindness. He pursues his foes, yet he is a refuge for those who trust him. His ways are unexplainable; he is not a tame God we can control or figure out. He is a lot like the lion character described by C. S. Lewis in *The Chronicles of Narnia*: "He isn't safe. But he's good. He's the King." How should we respond to such an almighty God? Love him, fear him—and trust his goodness!

💡 My Thoughts

What is my current concept of God? How does it match up
with the description in Nahum? _____

_____

_____

_____

_____

_____

💙 My Prayer

"Almighty, all-powerful God of the universe, praise and glory
belong to you alone! You are loving and kind. You are holy
and just. I confess I often try to put you in the box of my
own concept of you; yet you are unexplainable. You cannot
be contained! Thank you for your patience, kindness, and
mercy toward me. Help me to walk in a reverent fear of you
and find my refuge in your loving arms. In Jesus's name I
pray, amen."

This week I am praying for: _____

_____

_____

_____

_____

_____

Fearsome but Loving

 ## My Choices

- This week I will choose to see God as the all-powerful, untamable Lord over all creation.

- This week I will choose to see the mercy and patience of a loving and good God.

- This week I will choose to praise God for who he is and live in reverent fear of him.

- This week I will choose to: _____

_____

_____

_____

_____

_____

 **For Further Reading:** Psalms 104 and 105; Nahum 1

> There is in the awful
> and mysterious depths
> of the Triune God
> neither limit nor end.
>
> A. W. Tozer

Waiting on God's Timing

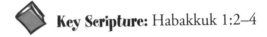

Key Scripture: Habakkuk 1:2–4

How long, O LORD, must I call for help,
  but you do not listen?
Or cry out to you, "Violence!"
  but you do not save?
Why do you make me look at injustice?
  Why do you tolerate wrong?
Destruction and violence are before me;
  there is strife, and conflict abounds.
Therefore the law is paralyzed,
  and justice never prevails.
The wicked hem in the righteous,
  so that justice is perverted.

God's plan will continue on God's schedule.

A. W. TOZER

Waiting on God's Timing

 **Reflection**

Are you sitting in God's waiting room? Perhaps you're waiting for an answer to a specific prayer. Perhaps you're waiting for a change in circumstances or a physical healing or spiritual revival in your church. Habakkuk had been waiting, and now he was at the end of his patience. Openly and honestly he approached God with his question: when was God going to do something about the wicked and rebellious people of Judah?

What was the Lord's answer? "Look at the nations and watch—and be utterly amazed. For I am going to do something in your days that you would not believe, even if you were told" (Habakkuk 1:5). God reassured Habakkuk that he was not ignoring the situation in Judah. On the contrary, he was at work in ways far beyond anything Habakkuk could imagine.

The same is true in our lives. God knows the big picture. He knows how and when he will allow everything to play out. What we want right now may not be the best thing for us right now. God has not closed his eyes to the situation; he has not forgotten us. During our waiting times, we have a choice: will we allow our faith to increase, or our stress? As we take our requests to God, let's approach him in faith. Let's trust his timing and find peace in the knowledge that he is at work in ways far beyond what we can see.

💡 My Thoughts

What requests do I need to hand over to God in faith while I patiently trust him for the answers? _____

_____

_____

_____

_____

_____

💜 My Prayer

"Wise and loving Father, I praise you, because you know all things and can do all things. I praise you for your love. You *are* love! I'm so thankful I can trust you, even in the waiting periods. I lay my request before you, asking you to work in a mighty way in my life. I believe you have a plan far bigger than anything I can even imagine. Help me rest in your sovereign care when I get impatient. Increase my faith! In Jesus's name I pray, amen."

This week I am praying for: _____

_____

_____

_____

_____

_____

Waiting on God's Timing

 My Choices

- This week I will choose to turn my stress to trust as I wait on the Lord's plan for my life.

- This week I will choose to recognize God's timing is better than my own.

- This week I will choose to remember God is at work, even when I can't see the results.

- This week I will choose to: _____

_____

_____

_____

_____

_____

 **For Further Reading:** Habakkuk 1–3; Psalm 37

> The man who measures things by
> the circumstances of the hour
> is filled with fear; the man
> who sees Jehovah enthroned
> and governing has no panic.
>
> G. CAMPBELL MORGAN

Heartfelt Joy

 **Key Scripture:** Zephaniah 3:14–17

Sing, O Daughter of Zion;
shout aloud, O Israel!
Be glad and rejoice with all your heart,
O Daughter of Jerusalem!
The LORD has taken away your punishment,
he has turned back your enemy.
The LORD, the King of Israel, is with you;
never again will you fear any harm.
On that day they will say to Jerusalem,
"Do not fear, O Zion;
do no let your hands hang limp.
The LORD your God is with you,
he is mighty to save.
He will take great delight in you,
he will quiet you with his love,
he will rejoice over you with singing."

Joy is not the absence of trouble but the presence of Christ.

WILLIAM VANDER HOVEN

Heartfelt Joy

 **Reflection**

Could there be any greater comfort than knowing the Lord your God takes great delight in you and will "quiet you with his love"? The Lord's superabundant love and care for his people make me stand in awe. Think of it: he knows our sins, our weaknesses, and our flaws, and yet he chooses to love us and even to delight in us. How great is our God! He is with us, and he is mighty to save us.

Dear friend, do you see his loving hand in your life? Do you know his grace and mercy? Turn to him, because of his great love for you. Run to him as your Savior and your King. Zephaniah brings a message of hope and joy to all who call upon the name of the Lord. May the comfort of this passage well up in our hearts and cause our lives to overflow with joy!

💡 My Thoughts

How do I see God's abundant love and comforting care at work in my life? _____

_____

_____

_____

_____

_____

💛 My Prayer

"Loving and merciful God, you are the Lord over heaven and earth. I praise you for your great love and care for me. I am humbled and amazed that you take delight in me. Thank you for your presence in my life. I rejoice in you! Help my life to reflect that joy, and may others be drawn to you as they see the comfort I have in you. In Jesus's name I pray, amen."

This week I am praying for: _____

_____

_____

_____

_____

_____

Heartfelt Joy

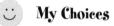 **My Choices**

- This week I will choose to rejoice because the Lord takes great delight in me and cares about my life.

- This week I will choose to share the truth about God's love with others.

- This week I will choose to thank the Lord for his presence in my life and ask him to calm my fears.

- This week I will choose to: _____

_____

_____

_____

_____

 **For Further Reading:** Zephaniah 3; Isaiah 54–55

Joy is not a luxury or a mere
accessory in the Christian life.
It is the sign that we are really
living in God's wonderful
love, and that love satisfies us.

ANDREW MURRAY

Busy Doing What?

 **Key Scripture:** Haggai 1:5–9

Now this is what the LORD Almighty says: "Give careful thought to your ways. You have planted much, but have harvested little. You eat, but never have enough. You drink, but never have your fill. You put on clothes, but are not warm. You earn wages, only to put them in a purse with holes in it."

This is what the LORD Almighty says: "Give careful thought to your ways. Go up into the mountains and bring down timber and build the house, so that I may take pleasure in it and be honored," says the LORD. "You expected much, but see, it turned out to be little. What you brought home, I blew away. Why?" declares the LORD Almighty. "Because of my house, which remains a ruin, while each of you is busy with his own house."

Only one life, 'twill soon be past.
Only what's done for Christ will last.

C. T. STUDD

Busy Doing What?

 **Reflection**

What keeps you busy? It's a fair question in a culture that seems to glorify busyness. Being busy is not bad in and of itself; but if we are busy doing things that distract us from what we ought to be doing, that is detrimental. Certain activities are necessary; others are a wise and important investment of our time; still other pursuits are a misuse of our time and energy. We need to discern the difference.

In today's passage God reprimanded his people, because they were too busy focusing on their own lives to think about the Lord. They spent all their time building their own homes and making their lives comfortable, while God's house sat in disrepair and ruin. God used the prophet Haggai to warn them it was time to reevaluate their priorities.

Perhaps it is time for us to rethink our priorities as well. God's call in Haggai is not an excuse to be lazy. It's not an excuse to ignore our responsibilities to our homes and families. Rather, it's a call to keep our priorities straight and our lives in balance. It's a call to work heartily as unto the Lord in everything we do. The question we must ask ourselves is, Are we investing quality time in God's kingdom, or are we too busy with our own little "kingdoms" to give any attention to his?

💡 My Thoughts

What changes do I need to make in my priorities and commitments? _____

_____

_____

_____

_____

_____

💛 My Prayer

"Glorious God, I praise you, for you alone are worthy of honor and praise. You are the almighty God and the high king of heaven. Thank you for the many blessings you have bestowed. You have been so good to me! Oh Lord, forgive me for the times when I have ignored your calling in my life. Forgive me for the times when I have gotten so busy I have forgotten your presence. Give me wisdom to keep my priorities in order and to honor you with my time. Thank you for gently leading me. In Jesus's name I pray, amen."

This week I am praying for: _____

_____

_____

_____

_____

_____

Busy Doing What?

 **My Choices**

- This week I will choose to examine my life and consider what keeps me busy.

- This week I will choose to reevaluate my priorities in light of what God wants me to do.

- This week I will choose to ask God to give me wisdom and direction in determining how I should spend my time.

- This week I will choose to: _____

_____

_____

_____

_____

For Further Reading: Haggai 1–2

> Busyness . . . feeds the ego but
> starves the inner man. It fills
> a calendar but fractures a
> family. It cultivates a program
> that plows under priorities.
>
> CHUCK SWINDOLL

How Should We Pray?

 Key Scripture: Matthew 6:9–13

"This, then, is how you should pray:
'Our Father in heaven,
hallowed be your name,
your kingdom come,
your will be done
on earth as it is in heaven.
Give us today our daily bread.
Forgive us our debts,
as we also have forgiven our debtors.
And lead us not into temptation,
but deliver us from the evil one.'"

Time spent in prayer is never wasted.

FRANÇOIS FENELON

How Should We Pray?

 **Reflection**

Jesus not only encouraged us to pray, he told us how to pray by giving us this example in Matthew 6. We begin with praise. Personally, I've found that beginning my morning and my prayer praising God for who he is and what he has accomplished is a wonderful way to start the new day! When we praise God, we recognize how magnificent and wise he is, and we acknowledge that there is nothing in our lives he can't handle. We experience relief from anxiety, knowing he is the Lord who knows all things and can do all things, and he loves us completely.

Our worries are further pacified as we take the next step: bringing our requests to him. Sometimes we may think something is too trivial to bring before almighty God, but look at Jesus's sample prayer: "Give us today our daily bread." He encourages us to give over the day's most basic needs to God's care.

Next, we ask for forgiveness, which reminds us to forgive others. Finally, we ask the Lord to lead us in the right direction, away from temptation and evil. Do you see how prayer not only blesses God, but changes us as well? Let's be devoted to prayer each day!

💡 My Thoughts

What is my prayer life like right now? What changes do I need to make in my life to devote myself more deeply to prayer?

_____

_____

_____

_____

_____

💗 My Prayer

"Wonderful and holy Father in heaven, I praise you, because you are the almighty, sovereign God. May your kingdom come soon, and may your will be done here on earth as it is in heaven. Please provide for my needs today. Help me to have the same grace and forgiveness toward others as you have toward me. Order my steps today, and direct me away from temptation. Deliver me from the evil one. In everything I do today, allow me to bring glory to you and you alone. In Jesus's name I pray, amen."

This week I am praying for: _____

_____

_____

_____

_____

_____

How Should We Pray?

☺ My Choices

- This week I will choose to begin each day praising the Lord for who he is and what he is able to do.

- This week I will choose to ask God to direct my steps and provide for me each day.

- This week I will choose to forgive others as I have been forgiven.

- This week I will choose to: _____

_____

_____

_____

_____

_____

 **For Further Reading:** Matthew 5–7

> Though we cannot by our
> prayers give God any
> information, yet we must by
> our prayers give him honor.
>
> MATTHEW HENRY

Take It to Heart

 **Key Scripture:** Mark 4:21–25

He [Jesus] said to them, "Do you bring in a lamp to put it under a bowl or a bed? Instead, don't you put it on its stand? For whatever is hidden is meant to be disclosed, and whatever is concealed is meant to be brought out into the open. If anyone has ears to hear, let him hear."

"Consider carefully what you hear," he continued. "With the measure you use, it will be measured to you—and even more. Whoever has will be given more; whoever does not have, even what he has will be taken from him."

Burying a talent is the betraying of a trust, and amounts to a forfeiture; and gifts and graces rust for want of wearing.

MATTHEW HENRY

Take It to Heart

 **Reflection**

In Jesus's time a lamp consisted of a lighted wick in a clay bowl filled with oil. It was typically placed on a stand to provide as much light as possible. Our passage today is surrounded by parables Jesus told his disciples in order to shed light on certain spiritual truths. He encouraged the disciples to carefully consider what they heard and take the truths to heart. He assured them as they did, they would eventually come to greater understanding: "Whoever has will be given more."

We, too, must carefully consider the spiritual truths we receive. As we listen to biblical teaching or read the Bible, what do we do with what we learn? Do we allow it to bounce right off our brains or do we absorb it, digest it, and allow it to change us? When we faithfully apply God's Word to our lives, we understand more and more. True spiritual growth takes place. But when we do nothing with the Word we have, it's as if we never had it. Our lamps are useless!

Dear friend, what are you doing with the biblical knowledge you have? Let's make sure we're putting God's Word into practice in our lives—and sharing it with others.

💡 My Thoughts

Am I applying the spiritual truths I know from God's Word?
Am I sharing them with the people in my life?

_____

_____

_____

_____

_____

♡ My Prayer

"Faithful and glorious Lord, I praise you, for your words
are powerful and true. Thank you for giving us the Bible,
so we can know how to live according to your ways. May
your Word be a lamp to my feet and a light along my path!
Oh Lord, I confess I have not always paid attention to your
truths or put them into practice. Open my eyes, unplug my
ears, and give me understanding. Help me to apply your
words to my life, so I may grow closer and closer to you. In
Jesus's name I pray, amen."

This week I am praying for: _____

_____

_____

_____

_____

_____

Take It to Heart

 ## My Choices

- This week I will choose to read God's Word faithfully.

- This week I will choose to apply the spiritual truths I learn to my life.

- This week I will choose to share God's truth with others.

- This week I will choose to: _____

_____

_____

_____

_____

For Further Reading: Mark 4; Psalm 119

The Christians who have
turned the world upside
down have been men
and women with a vision
in their hearts and the
Bible in their hands.

T. B. Maston

Jesus Still Calms Storms

 **Key Scripture:** Luke 8:22–25

One day Jesus said to his disciples, "Let's go over to the other side of the lake." So they got into a boat and set out. As they sailed, he fell asleep. A squall came down on the lake, so that the boat was being swamped, and they were in great danger.

The disciples went and woke him, saying, "Master, Master, we're going to drown!"

He got up and rebuked the wind and the raging waters; the storm subsided, and all was calm. "Where is your faith?" he asked his disciples.

In fear and amazement they asked one another, "Who is this? He commands even the winds and the water, and they obey him."

As sure as God puts his children in the furnace, He will be in the furnace with them.

CHARLES H. SPURGEON

Jesus Still Calms Storms

 **Reflection**

The disciples in the little boat were in great danger, tossing on the waves and frantically bailing water in the middle of a raging storm. Fear overtook them—while Jesus slept. Imagine that! Jesus was sleeping while they were fretting. They didn't understand that since Jesus was in the boat with them, they didn't have to worry. All they had to do was wake him up.

Isn't it funny how we sometimes wait and call on Jesus as a last resort, instead of going to him first? Jesus was the answer to the disciples' problem. He created the wind and the sea, and he was able to calm them both with a single rebuke. His one question to the disciples was, "Where is your faith?" They had placed their faith in the capacity of the boat, not in the Lord who was with them in the boat.

When the storms of life come—and they will—we must ask ourselves, "Where is our faith?" Is it in people or circumstances or our own abilities? Or is it in the mighty, all-powerful God? Will we go to him at the first rumblings of a storm, or will we go to him as a last resort?

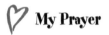 My Thoughts

How do I show my trust in Christ during the storms of life?

_____

_____

_____

_____

_____

♡ My Prayer

"Great and mighty God of all creation, I praise you, for you are my shelter. You are my rock and my refuge. You are my provider and my protector. Thank you for being with me through the good times and through the storms in life. I believe you are able to handle every difficulty and calm every storm. Help me to remember to turn to you first, at the first sign of trouble, instead of waiting until I am nearly swamped. Increase my faith as I look to you for help. In Jesus's name I pray, amen."

This week I am praying for: _____

_____

_____

_____

_____

_____

Jesus Still Calms Storms

 My Choices

- This week I will choose to pray to God rather than fret and worry when challenges arise.

- This week I will choose to trust Jesus to calm the storms in my life.

- This week I will choose to encourage others to call out to Jesus in the midst of their storms.

- This week I will choose to: _____

_____

_____

_____

_____

_____

 **For Further Reading:** Luke 8:26–56;
Isaiah 43:1–3

> Anyone who has the firm
> conviction that he will never be
> forsaken by the Lord will not be
> unduly anxious, because he will
> depend on His providence.
>
> JOHN CALVIN

Abide in Christ

 **Key Scripture:** John 15:1–5

"I am the true vine, and my Father is the gardener. He cuts off every branch in me that bears no fruit, while every branch that does bear fruit he prunes so that it will be even more fruitful. You are already clean because of the word I have spoken to you. Remain in me, and I will remain in you. No branch can bear fruit by itself; it must remain in the vine. Neither can you bear fruit unless you remain in me.

"I am the vine; you are the branches. If a man remains in me and I in him, he will bear much fruit; apart from me you can do nothing."

Live near to God, and all things will appear little to you in comparison with eternal realities.

ROBERT MURRAY M'CHEYNE

Abide in Christ

 **Reflection**

"Remaining in Christ" sounds heavenly and beautiful, but what does it really mean? How does a person "*remain in Jesus*"? Some Bible translations replace the word *remain* with *abide* or *dwell*. The meaning comes down to living in Christ continually.

I'm reminded of Paul's words to the early Christians, "Pray without ceasing" (1 Thessalonians 5:17 NKJV). That verse doesn't mean stopping life in order to sit and pray in a dark, lonely room 24/7. It does mean remaining in an attitude of prayer throughout the day, recognizing that God is with us and enjoying his presence.

Remaining or abiding in Christ means having an attitude of heart and mind that looks to Jesus throughout the day and chooses to seek refuge in him. It doesn't mean doing more "religious" activities; rather, it means practicing his presence and consciously remaining in his care. It means a life hidden in Christ. Basically, we have three choices: abiding in Christ, living independently in our own strength, or deliberately running the opposite way. Let's choose to turn our hearts and minds continually toward Jesus and know the joy and comfort of abiding in his presence!

💡 My Thoughts

Am I remaining (abiding, dwelling) in Christ, or am I going my own way and doing my own thing? _____

_____

_____

_____

_____

_____

♡ My Prayer

"Great and wonderful Father, I praise you for your constant presence in my life. Thank you for being the Great Gardener. Help me to remain in Christ, so that I may bear much fruit for your glory. I know I am only a branch; my life depends upon your sustenance and strength. Draw me to yourself and hold me there. I want to enjoy your presence all day long! Teach me to abide in your love, under the shelter of your wings. In Jesus's name I pray, amen."

This week I am praying for: _____

_____

_____

_____

_____

_____

Abide in Christ

 My Choices

- This week I will choose to reflect on God's goodness continually throughout each day.
- This week I will choose to pray without ceasing, recognizing God's presence in my life.
- This week I will choose to abide in God's Word and glorify him in everything I say and do.
- This week I will choose to: _____
  _____
  _____
  _____
  _____
  _____

 **For Further Reading:** John 15–16

> We must live a life of communion
> with God, even while our
> conversation is with the world.
>
> MATTHEW HENRY

There Is Always Hope

 **Key Scripture:** Acts 9:1–6

Meanwhile, Saul was still breathing out murderous threats against the Lord's disciples. He went to the high priest and asked him for letters to the synagogues in Damascus, so that if he found any there who belonged to the Way, whether men or women, he might take them as prisoners to Jerusalem. As he neared Damascus on his journey, suddenly a light from heaven flashed around him. He fell to the ground and heard a voice say to him, "Saul, Saul, why do you persecute me?"

"Who are you, Lord?" Saul asked.

"I am Jesus, whom you are persecuting," he replied. "Now get up and go into the city, and you will be told what you must do."

The word "hope" I take for faith; and indeed hope is nothing else but the constancy of faith.

JOHN CALVIN

There Is Always Hope

 **Reflection**

A life-changing journey, to say the least! Saul fought passionately against the followers of Jesus. Most Christians at that time would have considered him one of the least likely people to ever become a believer. But God knew better. Saul set out on the road to Damascus to persecute Christians; he arrived in Damascus as a new and humble Christian. Saul became the apostle Paul, and the archenemy of Christianity became its strongest proponent.

Have you ever thought someone you know is so spiritually lost, he or she will never come to know Jesus? Our story today gives us hope that even the most hard-hearted person can become a new creation in Christ. Never underestimate the transforming power of Christ as he draws hearts to himself. Don't give up hope! Instead, pray, knowing all things are possible with God. Let's trust his ways and his timing. He is more than able to open the eyes of the blind to see his love and the ears of the deaf to hear his beautiful voice.

Week 37

💡 My Thoughts

Is there someone in my life who needs to know the transforming power of Christ? Am I willing to faithfully pray for that person?_____

_____

_____

_____

_____

♡ My Prayer

"Powerful and mighty God, you are awesome and wonderful. Jesus, I praise you for willingly laying down your life for me on the cross. Thank you for saving me, a sinner, and transforming my life. Thank you for allowing me to be a partaker of your grace. Oh Lord, I pray for my friends and family members who need your presence in their lives. Please reveal yourself to them. Open their spiritual eyes and ears. Help me to faithfully share the power of your transforming love. In Jesus's name I pray, amen."

This week I am praying for: _____

_____

_____

_____

_____

_____

There Is Always Hope

 ## My Choices

- This week I will choose to thank the Lord for the transforming work he has done and continues to do in my life.

- This week I will choose to see the hope and potential in each person I meet.

- This week I will choose to pray for others and share Christ's redeeming message with them.

- This week I will choose to: _____

_____

_____

_____

_____

 **For Further Reading:** Acts 9–10

Dear Lord, what heavenly wonders
dwell in thy atoning blood!
By this are sinners snatched from
hell, and rebels brought to God.

ANNE STEELE

Living Sacrifice, Transformed Thinking

 **Key Scripture:** Romans 12:1–2

I urge you, brothers, in view of God's mercy, to offer your bodies as living sacrifices, holy and pleasing to God—this is your spiritual act of worship. Do not conform any longer to the pattern of this world, but be transformed by the renewing of your mind. Then you will be able to test and approve what God's will is—his good, pleasing and perfect will.

True conversion is the heart turning from Satan's control to God's, from sin to holiness, from the world to Christ.

ARTHUR W. PINK

Living Sacrifice, Transformed Thinking

 ## Reflection

I've heard it said, "The problem with 'living sacrifices' is that they keep getting up and crawling off the altar." Honestly, it's not easy to be a living sacrifice day in and day out. Yet, according to today's Scripture passage, that's exactly what we're called to do!

Submitting ourselves to Christ as living sacrifices is a spiritual act of worship. On a practical level it requires us to change some old and comfortable ways of living and thinking. Our pattern is no longer the world; it's Jesus. We need to think and act less as the world does and more like him. How? By renewing our minds—by allowing old patterns of thinking (such as anger, bitterness, worry, envy, lust, self-confidence) to give way to new, more Christlike patterns of love, forgiveness, peace, goodness, and confidence in God. As we begin to think differently, our words and actions will no longer conform to the world's image. Rather, in thought, word, and deed, we will become a reflection of Christ to the world.

Week 38

💡 My Thoughts

What changes do I need to make in the way I think in order to conform to the image of Christ?_____

_____

_____

_____

_____

_____

💗 My Prayer

"Holy and tender God, I praise you for offering your Son as a sacrifice for my sins. Thank you that I am a new creation in you. Help me to offer my whole life to you as a spiritual act of worship. Change my old, negative patterns of thinking and renew my mind, so I may live according to your Word and reflect Jesus to the world around me. In Jesus's name I pray, amen."

This week I am praying for: _____

_____

_____

_____

_____

_____

Living Sacrifice, Transformed Thinking

 My Choices

- This week I will choose to live my life as a living sacrifice to God.

- This week I will choose to ask God to show me the ways I am conforming to the world, rather than conforming to Christ.

- This week I will choose to be transformed by the renewing of my mind.

- This week I will choose to: _____

  _____

  _____

  _____

  _____

  _____

 **For Further Reading:** Romans 8–9; 12

> A religion that costs nothing
> is worth nothing!
>
> J. C. RYLE

The Fruit-Filled Life

 **Key Scripture:** Galatians 5:22–26

But the fruit of the Spirit is love, joy, peace, patience, kindness, goodness, faithfulness, gentleness and self-control. Against such things there is no law. Those who belong to Christ Jesus have crucified the sinful nature with its passions and desires. Since we live by the Spirit, let us keep in step with the Spirit. Let us not become conceited, provoking and envying each other.

As the soul does not live idly in the body, but gives motion and vigor to every member and part, so the Spirit of God cannot dwell in us without manifesting himself by the outward effects.

JOHN CALVIN

The Fruit-Filled Life

 ## Reflection

The fruit of God's Spirit is both lovely and flavorful. Who can deny the beauty of love, joy, peace, patience, kindness, and goodness in a woman's life? The interesting thing is, we can't take credit for our fruit, because it's not ours; we didn't produce it. We're just the branches that bear the fruit. (Remember week 36?) God produces the fruit as we walk in step with the Holy Spirit and follow his leadership in our lives—that is, as we seek his direction through prayer, listen to his voice through God's Word, and follow him in obedient action.

Dear friend, do you desire to bear the beautiful fruit of the Holy Spirit? As Christians we have been given the Holy Spirit in our lives. Let's not work against him by going our own way; instead let's walk in step with him, so that our lives overflow with love, joy, peace, patience, and every other spiritual fruit in abundance.

Week 39

💡 My Thoughts

Am I walking in step with the Holy Spirit? What fruit can others see in my life?_____

_____

_____

_____

_____

_____

💗 My Prayer

"Glorious and beautiful Lord, I praise you, because you are God, three in one—Father, Son, and Holy Spirit. Thank you for the gift of your Holy Spirit, who leads me, guides me, and comforts me. Thank you for transforming me in a powerful way to produce beautiful fruit in my life. Help me to walk in step with your Spirit and follow his lead. Allow me to bear fruit in abundance so that I may bring glory and honor to you. In Jesus's name I pray, amen."

This week I am praying for: _____

_____

_____

_____

_____

_____

The Fruit-Filled Life

 ## My Choices

- This week I will choose to thank God for his Holy Spirit and praise him for the fruit that is growing in my life.

- This week I will choose to follow the leading of the Holy Spirit and walk in step with him.

- This week I will choose to pray for the Holy Spirit to work in a powerful way through me.

- This week I will choose to: _____
_____
_____
_____
_____
_____

 **For Further Reading:** Galatians 4–6

> Our Lord never thought of a
> relationship to him that does not
> issue in fruitfulness for him.
>
> VANCE HAVNER

Spiritual Battle

 **Key Scripture:** Ephesians 6:10–13

Finally, be strong in the Lord and in his mighty power. Put on the full armor of God so that you can take your stand against the devil's schemes. For our struggle is not against flesh and blood, but against the rulers, against the authorities, against the powers of this dark world and against the spiritual forces of evil in the heavenly realms. Therefore put on the full armor of God, so that when the day of evil comes, you may be able to stand your ground, and after you have done everything, to stand.

There is no need for ignorance concerning the devices of the devil, for they are set forth plainly in the Word of God, and they are also visible all around us.

DONALD GREY BARNHOUSE

Spiritual Battle

 **Reflection**

A battle rages in the spiritual realm. Paul warns us to be aware of Satan's schemes and be strong in God's mighty power. Notice, he doesn't tell us to be strong in ourselves, but rather in the Lord. It's God's power alone that can withstand the enemy and bring victory in our lives.

Paul tells us to put on the full armor of God from head to toe: the belt of truth, the breastplate of righteousness, feet fitted with the readiness of the gospel of peace, the shield of faith, the helmet of salvation, and the sword of the Spirit (which is the Word of God). Where is the equipping room? It is the place of personal prayer and Bible study. As we draw close to God through prayer and the study and application of his Word, we become fully equipped for battle. Adorned with God's glorious armor, we are able to stand our ground and defeat the enemy—not in our own might, but in the Lord's.

Week 40

💡 My Thoughts

How do I prepare for spiritual battle? Am I spending time in the equipping room of prayer and Bible study?

_____

_____

_____

_____

_____

💗 My Prayer

"Great and mighty God, you alone have all authority over heaven and earth. Thank you for giving me your armor to face the spiritual battles of life. Oh Lord, equip me with the belt of truth, the breastplate of righteousness, the gospel of peace, the shield of faith, and the helmet of salvation. Teach me to faithfully wield the sword of your Spirit, which is your Word, the Bible. Give me your strength to stand against the devil's schemes. I know the ultimate victory is in your hands. In Jesus's name I pray, amen."

This week I am praying for: _____

_____

_____

_____

_____

_____

Spiritual Battle

 My Choices

- This week I will choose to prepare for spiritual battle through prayer.

- This week I will choose to equip myself by studying God's Word.

- This week I will choose to begin memorizing Scripture verses, so I will have the sword of the Spirit with me at all times.

- This week I will choose to: _____

_____

_____

_____

_____

_____

 **For Further Reading:** Ephesians 4–6

The devil's greatest asset is
the doubt people have
about his existence.

JOHN NICOLA

Press On!

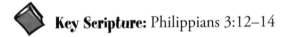 **Key Scripture:** Philippians 3:12–14

Not that I have already obtained all this, or have already been made perfect, but I press on to take hold of that for which Christ Jesus took hold of me. Brothers, I do not consider myself yet to have taken hold of it. But one thing I do: Forgetting what is behind and straining toward what is ahead. I press on toward the goal to win the prize for which God has called me heavenward in Christ Jesus.

The great thing in this world is not so much where you stand, as in what direction you are moving.

OLIVER WENDELL HOLMES

Press On!

Reflection

Instead of wallowing in regret about what he had done in the past, Paul chose to press forward toward the plan God had for him. If only we would do the same! It's so easy for us to ponder, dwell on, and rehearse the past. Maybe we're frustrated over mistakes we have made, bitter toward someone who has wronged us, or angry about a difficult childhood. If we continue to live in the past, we will be imprisoned by it. We won't be able to move forward and fulfill God's plan for our lives.

It's OK to recognize past pain, but we must not "live there." God has called us to a greater purpose. We must close the door on past mistakes, shortcomings, and failures, and look ahead to the powerful work God has called us to accomplish for his glory. I'm so glad Paul chose to forget the past and press forward toward his calling, aren't you? Let's do the same. It's time to move out of the prison of the past and focus on the beautiful work our redeeming Lord wants to do in our lives.

💡 My Thoughts

What regrets or pain from the past do I need to release? What steps do I need to take to move forward in my life?

_____

_____

_____

_____

_____

💗 My Prayer

"Redeeming and restoring Lord, you are able to do all things. Thank you for taking my past, my sin, and my shame, and forgiving me through Christ's blood. Thank you for making all things new. Thank you for working everything, including my past, together for the good. Help me close the door on the past, so I may press on to the new place you want me to go. Help me to fulfill my calling in you. Do a powerful work in my life so that I may glorify and honor you in all that I do. In Jesus's name I pray, amen."

This week I am praying for: _____

_____

_____

_____

_____

_____

Press On!

:) **My Choices**

- This week I will choose to stop wallowing in the past events of my life.

- This week I will choose to step forward into what God has called me to do.

- This week I will choose to forgive anyone against whom I hold a past grudge.

- This week I will choose to: _____

_____

_____

_____

_____

_____

 **For Further Reading:** Philippians 2–4

> Many intelligent adults are
> restrained in thoughts,
> actions, and results.
> They never move further
> than the boundaries of
> their self-imposed limitation.
>
> JOHN C. MAXWELL

Peace, Gratitude, and Wisdom

 **Key Scripture:** Colossians 3:15–17

Let the peace of Christ rule in your hearts, since as members of one body you were called to peace. And be thankful. Let the word of Christ dwell in you richly as you teach and admonish one another with all wisdom, and as you sing psalms, hymns and spiritual songs with gratitude in your hearts to God. And whatever you do, whether in word or deed, do it all in the name of the Lord Jesus, giving thanks to God the Father through him.

We sleep in peace in the arms of God when we yield ourselves up to his providence.

FRANÇOIS FENELON

Peace, Gratitude, and Wisdom

 **Reflection**

Have you ever wished you could take a "positive pill"? Here it is in one simple dose! It's so easy for us to take a "cup half-empty" attitude toward life. Thankfully, today's passage offers the perfect medicine for developing a more upbeat attitude.

First, we must let Christ's peace (not our own sense of peace) rule our hearts. The word *rule* comes from the Greek term used to describe an umpire or referee. When storms and troubles come, instead of looking to our own answers to "umpire" our hearts, we must allow Christ and his peace to take over and rule. Next, we must be thankful. A thankful heart focuses upward and looks for what is good in a situation. Thankfulness takes our eyes off the negatives and dispels our fears. Finally, we must allow God's Word to dwell in us richly. When our hearts are filled with God's wisdom and truth, we are less likely to dwell in hopelessness or despair. Instead, we are able to gain reassurance and hope as we focus on what the Bible says about God's great power and love.

So here's your "positive pill" for each day: Let Christ's peace rule your heart. Choose to be thankful. Dwell on God's Word. By following this prescription, your cup will be more than half-full. It will be overflowing!

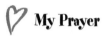 My Thoughts

How can I apply these three positive principles in my life?

_____

_____

_____

_____

_____

♡ My Prayer

"Marvelous and loving God, I praise you for your goodness. Thank you for the many ways in which you have blessed me. Thank you for the special people in my life. Thank you for what you are doing in the circumstances of my life. Help me to see the positive, even when things are challenging or difficult. Wonderful Lord, I ask for your peace to referee my heart. Help me to keep my eyes on you, and dispel all my fears! Draw me to the great truth found in your Word, and help me to find my strength and comfort there. In Jesus's name I pray, amen."

This week I am praying for: _____

_____

_____

_____

_____

_____

Peace, Gratitude, and Wisdom

 My Choices

- This week I will choose to let the peace of Christ rule my heart, especially when I am facing turmoil or difficulty.
- This week I will choose to have a continually thankful attitude.
- This week I will choose to let God's Word dwell richly in my life by reading, studying, and memorizing Scripture.
- This week I will choose to: _____

_____

_____

_____

_____

_____

 **For Further Reading:** Colossians 2–4

In thanking God, we fasten upon
his favors to us; in praising and
adoring God, we fasten upon his
perfections in himself.

MATTHEW HENRY

Encouragement from the Lord

 **Key Scripture:** 2 Thessalonians 2:15–17

So then, brothers, stand firm and hold to the teachings we passed on to you, whether by word of mouth or by letter.

May our Lord Jesus Christ himself and God our Father, who loved us and by his grace gave us eternal encouragement and good hope, encourage your hearts and strengthen you in every good deed and word.

Encouragement is oxygen to the soul.

GEORGE M. ADAMS

Encouragement from the Lord

 ## Reflection

Encouragement from a friend is nice. An encouraging word from a family member is even better. But encouragement from God is amazing! As a recipient of God's love and grace, Paul received "eternal encouragement" and "good hope" from God himself. He wanted that same encouragement and hope for his fellow Christians.

The word *encourage* means to give strength to the heart. Often we seek encouragement and positive words from the people around us. The impact of those words, however, can be temporary and possibly disappointing. On the other hand, God's encouragement is strong, fulfilling, and eternal, spurring us on to good words and deeds. It gives long-lasting strength to our hearts. What does God's encouragement look like? It may come in the form of a confident, internal assurance that the Lord is with us. We may feel his good pleasure in what we are doing. He may lead us to a strengthening verse in the Bible or bring a person into our lives to speak a message of encouragement to our weary souls.

Let's keep our eyes and ears open for an encouraging word from our heavenly Father this week. He alone can bring eternal encouragement, hope, and strength to our hearts.

💡 My Thoughts

How has the Lord given me encouragement, hope, and strength at different times in my life? _____

_____

_____

_____

_____

_____

🖤 My Prayer

"Loving and wonderful God, you are the Great Encourager. Thank you for the way you are able to strengthen my heart. You alone refresh my spirit! Oh Lord, I need your encouragement and hope as I go about my daily tasks. I look to you to give me the strength I need for this day. Allow me to feel your presence and your pleasure as I seek to walk in your ways. Lead me to be an encourager to others. In Jesus's name I pray, amen."

This week I am praying for: _____

_____

_____

_____

_____

_____

Encouragement from the Lord

 My Choices

- This week I will choose to look to the Lord for true and eternal encouragement.
- This week I will choose to look to God's Word to receive strength for my soul.
- This week I will choose to be a vessel of God's encouragement to others.
- This week I will choose to: _____

_____

_____

_____

_____

_____

 **For Further Reading:** 2 Thessalonians 1–3

> When the outlook is dark, and the
> in-look's discouraging,
> just try the up-look;
> it's always encouraging.
>
> AUTHOR UNKNOWN

The Treasure of God's Word

 **Key Scripture:** 2 Timothy 3:14–17

But as for you, continue in what you have learned and have become convinced of, because you know those from whom you learned it, and how from infancy you have known the holy Scriptures, which are able to make you wise for salvation through faith in Christ Jesus. All Scripture is God-breathed and is useful for teaching, rebuking, correcting and training in righteousness, so that the man of God may be thoroughly equipped for every good work.

God's Word is such perfect truth and righteousness that it needs no patching or repair; in its course it makes a perfectly straight line, without any bends in any direction.

MARTIN LUTHER

The Treasure of God's Word

 **Reflection**

Never underestimate the power of God's Word in your life! The Bible is truly God-breathed and holds the words of life for each of us. In this one book, we find our foundation of truth and wisdom; our source of love, hope, and encouragement; and the equipping we need to do the good works God has called us to do. Never out of date, it continues to teach, rebuke, correct, and train us, as we faithfully read and study its pages.

Personally, I have found the Bible to be the one sure foundation for my understanding of who God is and what his character is like. It is the final authority in my life. When people question the validity of the Scriptures, I implore them to read the Bible for themselves and search for the truth God reveals through his living Word. I don't have to defend the Bible; it defends itself, as readers discover God's amazing love and timeless wisdom. May we never ignore so great a treasure!

💡 My Thoughts

Am I a student of God's Word? In what ways am I continuing to learn from the Bible? _____

_____

_____

_____

_____

_____

💗 My Prayer

"Wise and holy God, I praise you for the power of your Word. Thank you for the Holy Scriptures, by which I can come to know you better and learn to walk in your ways. Thank you for teaching me, rebuking me, correcting me, and training me through the words of the Bible. Help me to be faithful to read, study, and meditate on this amazing treasure, and lead me to apply its truths to my daily life. In Jesus's name I pray, amen."

This week I am praying for: _____

_____

_____

_____

_____

_____

The Treasure of God's Word

 My Choices

- This week I will choose to read God's Word and meditate on its truth.

- This week I will choose to apply what I learn from the Bible to my daily living.

- This week I will choose to be open to any rebuke or correction I receive from God through his Word.

- This week I will choose to: _____

_____

_____

_____

_____

_____

 **For Further Reading:** 2 Timothy 1–4

> We must read our Bibles like men
> digging for hidden treasure.
>
> J. C. RYLE

Precious Grace

 **Key Scripture:** Titus 3:4–7

But when the kindness and love of God our Savior appeared, he saved us, not because of righteous things we had done, but because of his mercy. He saved us through the washing of rebirth and renewal by the Holy Spirit, whom he poured out on us generously through Jesus Christ our Savior, so that, having been justified by his grace, we might become heirs having the hope of eternal life.

Perfection demands perfection; that is why salvation must be by grace, and why works are not sufficient.

DONALD GREY BARNHOUSE

Precious Grace

 **Reflection**

If we're good swimmers, we may be able to swim across an Olympic-sized pool in our own strength and ability. But the ocean? That's a different story! There is no way we can swim across that vast and great divide in our own power and strength.

Spiritually speaking, it's tempting to think we can cross the great divide between sinful man and a holy God by doing good deeds or works of mercy and righteousness. Our passage today gives us this grace-filled reminder: no way! It is not by our acts of righteousness but rather by God's generous mercy we are saved. We don't inherit the kingdom of heaven based on our own merit; if we did, we would have reason to be prideful. Rather, we are justified by God's grace through Jesus Christ our Savior. It is his work, not ours, that saves.

Trying to earn our way to heaven through our own good deeds is like trying to swim across the ocean in our own strength. Jesus Christ is the lifeboat sent by our merciful God to rescue us from the penalty of sin. Only by faith do we get on board.

💡 My Thoughts

Am I trying to earn my own salvation, or do I recognize that God has provided salvation through his Son, Jesus Christ?

_____

_____

_____

_____

_____

💗 My Prayer

"Loving Lord and gracious heavenly Father, I praise you for your generous mercy. I confess I've been tempted to think I can work my way to salvation. I've been tempted to think I can earn a place in heaven through my own strength and ability. But even my best efforts, I know, are woefully inadequate! Thank you that by your grace I am saved, through faith in your Son, Jesus. Help me to walk humbly and thankfully in the beauty of your great kindness, mercy, and love. In Jesus's name I pray, amen."

This week I am praying for: _____

_____

_____

_____

_____

_____

Precious Grace

 ## My Choices

- This week I will choose to thank the Lord for his grace and mercy toward me.

- This week I will choose to live each day by faith, not in my own ability, but in God's.

- This week I will choose to recognize and appreciate the hope of eternal life I have through Christ.

- This week I will choose to: _____

_____

_____

_____

_____

_____

 **For Further Reading:** Titus 1–3

> All that I was, my sin, my guilt, my
> death, was all my own;
> All that I am I owe to Thee, my
> gracious God, alone.

HORATIUS BONAR

Formerly Useless, Now Useful

 **Key Scripture:** Philemon 8–12

Therefore, although in Christ I could be bold and order you to do what you ought to do, yet I appeal to you on the basis of love. I then, as Paul—an old man and now also a prisoner of Christ Jesus—I appeal to you for my son Onesimus, who became my son while I was in chains. Formerly he was useless to you, but now he has become useful both to you and to me.

I am sending him—who is my very heart—back to you.

We are not to think that, where we see no possibility, God sees none.

MARCUS DODS

Formerly Useless, Now Useful

 **Reflection**

What truth can we possibly glean from this little note sent from Paul to a slave owner named Philemon? Paul was writing on behalf of a runaway slave named Onesimus, asking Philemon to graciously receive him back. As a fugitive slave, Onesimus had become a follower of Christ and had ministered to the needs of Paul while he was in prison. Paul acknowledged that Onesimus (whose name means "profitable") was once useless to his owner, but now he had become useful. What made the difference? The transforming power of Christ! Through Jesus, God had changed a runaway slave into a renewed creature—a rebellious attitude into a serving spirit. He made the useless useful!

We learn a powerful lesson from this short letter: don't give up on anyone or underestimate what God can do in a person's life. After all, each one of us was a fugitive from God's love before we knew Jesus. God chose to save us by his grace. Now we, as Onesimus, are new creatures in Christ. Once we were useless; now we are useful. May his transforming power continue to do its work in our lives!

Week 46

💡 My Thoughts

What positive changes has God made in my life since I have come to know Jesus?_____

_____

_____

_____

_____

_____

💛 My Prayer

"Glorious Redeemer, you are an awesome and marvelous God. Nothing is impossible for you. You are able to take a reckless sinner like me and transform her into a beautiful new creature. Thank you for your renewing power and redeeming love. Please continue your transforming work in my life. Allow me to grow and change so that I may become more useful in your kingdom. Weed out the useless qualities in my character, and plant seeds of faith, hope, and love in their place. In Jesus's name I pray, amen."

This week I am praying for: _____

_____

_____

_____

_____

_____

Formerly Useless, Now Useful

 My Choices

- This week I will choose to pray for God's transforming power in my life.

- This week I will choose to see the positive potential in the lives of the people around me.

- This week I will choose to encourage others in their faith, recognizing that each of us is a work in progress.

- This week I will choose to: _____
  _____
  _____
  _____
  _____
  _____

 For Further Reading: Philemon 1–25 and
2 Corinthians 5

> The same power that brought
> Christ back from the dead
> is operative within those who
> are Christ's. The Resurrection
> is an ongoing thing.
>
> LEON MORRIS

Running with Endurance

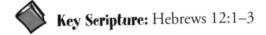 **Key Scripture:** Hebrews 12:1–3

Therefore, since we are surrounded by such a great cloud of witnesses, let us throw off everything that hinders and the sin that so easily entangles, and let us run with perseverance the race marked out for us. Let us fix our eyes on Jesus, the author and perfecter of our faith, who for the joy set before him endured the cross, scorning its shame, and sat down at the right hand of the throne of God. Consider him who endured such opposition from sinful men, so that you will not grow weary and lose heart.

Endurance is not just the ability to bear a hard thing, but to turn it into glory.

WILLIAM BARCLAY

Running with Endurance

 **Reflection**

Olympic runners make it look so easy. They're grace in motion. But they have become world-class athletes only through blood, sweat, and tears. They have endured the pain and agony of countless strenuous workouts, races, wins, and defeats. To achieve peak performance, they have learned to rid themselves of anything that could slow them down or throw them off balance. They have trained their eyes to focus on the finish line, knowing one glance at the crowd or the other runners may cost them the race.

Each of us is running a race too—the race of life. And it isn't easy! That's why Paul encourages us to run with endurance; get rid of any sins that hinder or entangle us; and keep the finish line—the Lord Jesus—in our sights. Dear friend, are you feeling weak, fainthearted, ready to quit the race? Fix your eyes on Jesus, the one who endured the cross, and ask him for direction and strength. He is our hero and the champion of our faith. With Jesus on our side, the victory is assured.

Week 47

💡 My Thoughts

What hurdles am I facing in my race of life? Am I keeping my eyes on Jesus? _____

_____

_____

_____

_____

_____

💜 My Prayer

"Precious Lord, loving Father, I praise you for your faithfulness toward me. Thank you that Jesus is the author and perfecter of my faith. I'm so grateful that he endured the cross on my behalf. Help me to persevere in the race of life you have set before me. Show me the sins I need to lay aside. Help me keep my eyes fixed on Jesus, not on people or circumstances. May my life reflect the joy of Christ, as I find my victory in him. In Jesus's name I pray, amen."

This week I am praying for: _____

_____

_____

_____

_____

_____

Running with Endurance

😊 **My Choices**

- This week I will choose to examine my life and get rid of those sins and entanglements that hinder my walk with Christ.

- This week I will choose to run with perseverance the race marked out for me.

- This week I will choose to fix my eyes on Jesus, recognizing him as the author and perfecter of my faith.

- This week I will choose to: _____

_____

_____

_____

_____

For Further Reading: Hebrews 11–13

> About the time we are ready to give up, Jesus comes alongside and whispers, "Don't quit, keep going, keep your eyes on Me," as He provides His gentle touch of grace, joy and love at just the right moment.
>
> CHUCK SWINDOLL

Taming the Tongue

 **Key Scripture:** James 1:26; 3:9–12

If anyone considers himself religious and yet does not keep a tight rein on his tongue, he deceives himself and his religion is worthless. . . .

With the tongue we praise our Lord and Father, and with it we curse men, who have been made in God's likeness. Out of the same mouth come praise and cursing. My brothers, this should not be. Can both fresh water and salt water flow from the same spring? My brothers, can a fig tree bear olives, or a grapevine bear figs? Neither can a salt spring produce fresh water.

Our words are the evidence of the state of our hearts, as surely as the taste of the water is an evidence of the state of the spring.

J. C. Ryle

Taming the Tongue

🌸 Reflection

Like an unbridled horse, our tongues can run wild, causing great injury and suffering in the process. According to today's passage, God cares about how we use our tongues. Are we using them to build up the people around us, or are we using them to inflict pain? Are we using them to speak good of others, or to speak ill?

Taming our own tongues is nearly impossible. Certainly, we must take responsibility for the words we speak, and we must do everything we can to guard our mouths. But ultimately, controlling the tongue requires a heart change—something that is possible only through the work of the Holy Spirit. You see, what pours out of the mouth is an overflow of what issues from the heart. If our hearts are filled with anger, resentment, and deceit, these characteristics will be spewed from our lips. If, however, our hearts are filled with thankfulness, love, and forgiveness, *these* characteristics will be evident in the words we speak.

To harness our tongues, we must allow the Holy Spirit to change our hearts. Starting today, let's pray with King David, "Create in me a clean heart, O God, and renew a steadfast spirit within me" (Psalm 51:10 NKJV).

Week 48

💡 My Thoughts

How do my words and conversations reflect the issues of my heart? _____

_____

_____

_____

_____

_____

💙 My Prayer

"Amazing and all-powerful God, I praise you for your Holy Spirit, who convicts me of sin and helps me live according to your Word. Lord, I confess I have misused my tongue. Too often the words I have spoken have been hurtful rather than helpful. Clean me on the inside and purify my heart. Do a powerful work in me so my heart and my conversation reflect only your love, kindness, mercy, and grace. In Jesus's name I pray, amen."

This week I am praying for: _____

_____

_____

_____

_____

_____

Taming the Tongue

 **My Choices**

- This week I will choose to seek God's help in using my tongue to encourage others.

- This week I will choose to turn from the sins of gossip, deceit, and unkind speech.

- This week I will choose to do a heart check and ask God to cleanse me in those areas that trigger my unruly tongue.

- This week I will choose to: _____

_____

_____

_____

_____

_____

For Further Reading: James 1–3

The real art of conversation is not
only to say the right thing
in the right place, but to leave
unsaid the wrong thing
at the tempting moment.

DOROTHY NEVILL

Love in Action

 **Key Scripture:** 1 Peter 4:8–11

Above all, love each other deeply, because love covers over a multitude of sins. Offer hospitality to one another without grumbling. Each one should use whatever gift he has received to serve others, faithfully administering God's grace in its various forms. If anyone speaks, he should do it as one speaking the very words of God. If anyone serves, he should do it with the strength God provides, so that in all things God may be praised through Jesus Christ. To him be the glory and the power for ever and ever. Amen.

Love never reasons, but profusely gives; gives, like a thoughtless prodigal, its all, and trembles then lest it has done too little.

HANNAH MORE

Love in Action

🌸 Reflection

Deeply loving others goes far beyond simply saying the words "I love you." Deeper love looks past faults and annoyances and is generous with forgiveness. It acts unselfishly, opening up heart and home in service to others.

The best way for us to love one another deeply is to use our gifts and talents for the benefit of the church, the body of Christ. God has given each of us specific gifts to use in service to his body; yet many times we hoard or misuse those gifts. What gift has God given you? Is it the gift of encouragement or teaching, mercy or discernment, hospitality or giving? Whatever our gifts and talents, let's offer them willingly, as an act of love and service toward God and his people. How beautiful is the body of Christ when we truly love one another!

Week 49

💡 My Thoughts

How am I showing love to others through my gifts and talents? _____

_____

_____

_____

_____

_____

💗 My Prayer

"Loving and gracious God, I praise you, because you are love. Thank you for demonstrating your great love for us by sending your Son, Jesus. Thank you for giving me gifts and talents that can be useful in the body of Christ. Help me to identify those gifts, and show me how to use them for your glory and to serve my brothers and sisters in Christ. Allow your great and abundant love to flow through me! In Jesus's name I pray, amen."

This week I am praying for: _____

_____

_____

_____

_____

_____

Love in Action

:-) My Choices

- This week I will choose to love people deeply and overlook faults and annoyances.

- This week I will choose to serve my brothers and sisters in Christ by using my gifts and talents.

- This week I will choose to show hospitality in big and small ways without grumbling.

- This week I will choose to: _____

_____

_____

_____

_____

_____

 **For Further Reading:** 1 Peter 4–5

> Nothing will be intentionally
> lacking where there is love.
>
> J. C. RYLE

Assurance of Eternal Life

 **Key Scripture:** 1 John 5:10–13

Anyone who believes in the Son of God has this testimony in his heart. Anyone who does not believe God has made him out to be a liar, because he has not believed the testimony God has given about his Son. And this is the testimony: God has given us eternal life, and this life is in his Son. He who has the Son has life; he who does not have the Son of God does not have life.

I write these things to you who believe in the name of the Son of God so that you may know that you have eternal life.

The faith that saves is not a conclusion drawn from evidence; it is a moral thing, a thing of the spirit, a supernatural infusion of confidence in Jesus Christ, a very gift of God.

A. W. TOZER

Assurance of Eternal Life

 **Reflection**

What does the Bible have to say about the connection between God's Son and eternal life? Here we see it spelled out quite clearly: God calls us to believe in Jesus Christ, his Son, and those of us who believe have eternal life. We don't have to play a guessing game; the Bible says we can know we have eternal life with assurance. Those who have the Son have eternal life, and those who don't have the Son don't have eternal life. It's that simple.

Some people say, "Oh, whatever works for you," or, "I believe there are many ways to heaven." But our Scripture passage today doesn't leave the truth open-ended. Eternal life is in the Son! Dear friend, let's examine our faith and make sure it's grounded on the solid rock of Jesus and the assurance of God's Word—not on current philosophies or people's latest whims. May we rest in the wonderful knowledge that because we have Jesus, we know we have eternal life.

Week 50

 **My Thoughts**

What do I believe about Jesus and eternal life?

_____

_____

_____

_____

_____

My Prayer

"Loving and forgiving God, thank you for your promise of eternal life through your Son, Jesus. Thank you for making the plan of salvation so plain and simple. Thank you that because I believe in Jesus and have him in my life, I am able to know without a doubt I have eternal life. Increase my faith, and help me to keep it grounded on the solid rock of your Word. Help me to rest in the assurance that I have eternal life through Jesus Christ. In Jesus's name I pray, amen."

This week I am praying for: _____

_____

_____

_____

_____

_____

Assurance of Eternal Life

 My Choices

- This week I will choose to believe eternal life is in the Son of God, not in any other person or philosophy.

- This week I will choose to rest in the assurance of my salvation through Christ.

- This week I will choose to tell others about the eternal life available through faith in God's Son, Jesus.

- This week I will choose to: _____

_____

_____

_____

_____

_____

For Further Reading: 1 John 4–5; John 3

> Jesus has made the life of His people as eternal as His own.
>
> CHARLES H. SPURGEON

Joyful Proclamation

 **Key Scripture:** Jude 24–25

To him who is able to keep you from falling and to present you before his glorious presence without fault and with great joy—to the only God our Savior be glory, majesty, power and authority, through Jesus Christ our Lord, before all ages, now and forevermore! Amen.

Here joy begins to enter into us, there we enter into joy.

THOMAS WATSON

Joyful Proclamation

 **Reflection**

Hope and joy well up in my heart as I read this well-known doxology. What could bring more comfort than knowing our Lord and Savior is able to keep us from falling? His hand holds us up. We may stumble, but we won't fall, because he cares for us. What's more, Jesus is able to present us without fault before God's glorious presence. He who gave his life on our behalf will present us to the Father with great joy!

Do you sense God's genuine and gracious love for you in this passage? Sometimes we become so familiar with certain Scripture verses, we fail to embrace the joy and comfort they offer. But wrapped up in this true and sincere praise of our wonderful God is the joyful revelation of his great compassion and care for us. Together let's joyfully proclaim his glory, majesty, power, and authority, both now and forevermore!

Week 51

💡 My Thoughts

Which attributes of the Lord bring joy to my heart?

_____

_____

_____

_____

_____

🤍 My Prayer

"Marvelous and wonderful God, I praise you, for there is none like you. You alone are the High King of heaven, the one true God. You are able to do all things, and by your power all things exist. I praise you for your sovereignty and your mercy. Thank you for your Son, Jesus, who gave his life on my behalf. Please, Lord, keep me from stumbling and falling, as I entrust my life into your loving hands. Help me to find joy in your presence and comfort in your loving arms. In Jesus's name I pray, amen."

This week I am praying for: _____

_____

_____

_____

_____

_____

Joyful Proclamation

 ## My Choices

- This week I will choose to reflect on the power and authority of the Lord.

- This week I will choose to take joy in the fact that he loves me and is able to keep me from falling.

- This week I will choose to live confidently in the assurance that one day Jesus will present me faultless and with great joy before God's throne.

- This week I will choose to: _____

_____

_____

_____

_____

_____

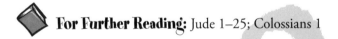 **For Further Reading:** Jude 1–25; Colossians 1

My God, how wonderful thou art!
Thy majesty how bright!
How beautiful thy mercy seat in
depths of burning light!

FREDERICK W. FABER

Passion or Playing?

 **Key Scripture:** Revelation 2:2–4

I know your deeds, your hard work and your perseverance. I know that you cannot tolerate wicked men, that you have tested those who claim to be apostles but are not, and have found them false. You have persevered and have endured hardships for my name, and have not grown weary.

Yet I hold this against you: You have forsaken your first love.

We are called to an everlasting preoccupation with God.

A. W. TOZER

Passion or Playing?

 **Reflection**

When we were kids, many of us loved to play "house." We dressed up like mommies, cuddled our dollies, and pretended to cook meals in our play kitchens. Now, as adult women, it's tempting for many of us to play "church." We dress up on Sundays, put smiles on our faces, go to all the important meetings, and serve when we can. There's a problem, though, when we mistake our "play" activities for a real relationship with Jesus Christ.

The words in our passage today were a message for the church at Ephesus, but they are words for us to heed as well. Are we simply going through the motions, doing what we think we're supposed to do to play "church"? Or are we passionate about Christ and growing in a love relationship with him? Jesus doesn't want our performance at church; he wants our hearts devoted to him in love. In Mark 12:30 he spells out our top priority: "Love the Lord your God with all your heart and with all your soul and with all your mind and with all your strength."

Dear friend, let's not forsake our first love! As we come to the end of this book and our time together, let's agree to stop playing "church." Instead, in the weeks and months ahead, let's pursue a real, authentic love relationship with Jesus Christ. Let's fall in love with Jesus all over again!

💡 My Thoughts

How would I describe my love relationship with Christ? Do I need to fall in love with Jesus all over again?

_____

_____

_____

_____

_____

💛 My Prayer

"Loving Father, I praise you for your kindness and mercy. You are a God of love. You are love! I am amazed at your grace and compassion toward me. Oh Lord, help my love for you to grow and grow. I want to pursue you with my whole heart. I want my love for you to be overflowing and genuine. Draw me to yourself. I desire only you. Refresh in me an undying love and devotion, so I may honor you with my life. In Jesus's name I pray, amen."

This week I am praying for: _____

_____

_____

_____

_____

_____

Passion or Playing?

 My Choices

- This week I will choose to return to my first love for Jesus by passionately pursuing a closer relationship with him.

- This week I will choose to relish and enjoy God's great love for me.

- This week I will choose to reexamine my life to determine what I am doing out of love for Christ and what I am doing out of duty or to play "church."

- This week I will choose to: _____

_____

_____

_____

_____

 **For Further Reading:** Revelation 1–3

> Talk with us, Lord, thyself reveal,
> while here on earth we rove;
> Speak to our hearts, and let us feel
> the kindling of thy love.
>
> CHARLES WESLEY

52 More Devotionals for the Positively Powerful Mom

THE Motherhood CLUB
Sharing a Difference One Mom at a Time
INC.

52 Monday Morning Motivations

THe P*wer oF A P☺sitive M♥M

Devotional & Journal

Karol Ladd

◆ HOWARD BOOKS
A DIVISION OF SIMON & SCHUSTER

Available where good books are sold • www.howardpublishing.com

Never Underestimate the Power of a Positive Woman!

In addition to Karol Ladd's inspirational devotionals, she also offers you five more ways to be a positive influence in the lives of those you love. One of the most amazing things about these books—the comment heard over and over—is that they share practical suggestions that are really doable!

Each of these books offers seven power-filled principles that will change the way you interact with others forever. In addition to these solid principles, each chapter includes four "Power Points":

- a *scripture* for you to read
- a *prayer* for power in your relationship
- a *verse* for you to memorize
- an *action step* to help you put your positive influence into action

Once you've read one, you'll want to read them all. You, too, can join the thousands of women who are becoming positive, powerful influences in the lives of their family and friends.

ISBN 1-4165-3358-3   ISBN 1-4165-3348-6   ISBN 1-4165-3362-1

ISBN 1-4165-3377-X   ISBN 1-4165-4141-1

HOWARD BOOKS
A DIVISION OF SIMON & SCHUSTER

Available where good books are sold • www.howardpublishing.com

ISBN 1-4165-4143-8

An Interactive Group Study
for Positive MOMS

Designed for a dynamic, interactive group study, these eight sessions will bring the power of a positive influence into the life of every woman who attends:

1. The Portrait of a Positive Mom
2. The Power of Encouragement
3. The Power of Prayer
4. The Power of a Good Attitude
5. The Power of Strong Relationships
6. The Power of Your Example
7. The Power of Strong Moral Standards
8. The Power of Love and Forgiveness

This easy-to-use DVD has been carefully designed so that anyone can facilitate a dynamic group session. No leadership training is needed.

The Power of a Positive Mom book complements the sessions on this DVD and is available wherever good books are sold.

www.howardpublishing.com

HOWARD BOOKS
A DIVISION OF SIMON & SCHUSTER